CONTENTS

4

INTRODUCTION

This guide is for those bioscientists teaching in higher education who are interested in using self- and peer-assessment in their learning and teaching activities, but who may feel they have little understanding of how to go about doing so. Some of the reasons for choosing self- and peer-assessment as opposed to other assessment methods are outlined in Table 1 on page 5.

This book is written to a specific format, made up of three chapters:

Chapter 1 is an introductory chapter that discusses some concerns about the most common assessment practices within higher education today. Through this under-standing, we can proceed towards illustrating how self- and peer-assessment can be a positive instrument for change. In order to be used effectively, it is helpful to understand the theoretical learning framework which underpins these student-centred assessment practices. Chapter 1 concludes with a discussion on effective learning through self- and peer-assessment. This chapter is very much about providing a rationale for the need for change and provides a way in which meaningful change can be brought about.

Chapter 2 considers in detail how you can get started with self- and peer-assessment. Specific issues related to the effective design, implementation and evaluation of self- and peer-assessment, such as the central role played by students engaging with marking criteria are discussed in detail. Here we take a deeper look at those requirements, from developing marking criteria to the development of a community of practice, providing practical suggestions in undertaking self- and peer-assessment, whilst illustrating some requirements for good practice.

Chapter 3 reflects the world in which students are being prepared. This is a world which requires the achievement of complex learning outcomes in order to meet the demands of employment and engagement in lifelong learning. Such learning outcomes are part-icularly well served by the application of self- and peer-assessment. The Chapter then moves from learning environments that use self- and peer-assessment, such as problem-based and reflective learning, to consider the role of formative and summative assessment and finally to considering how students and tutors perceive each assessment source.

The structure of the book is therefore to look at the rationale for using self- and peer-assessment, to outline effective application and finally to see how effective a learning tool both self- and peer-assessment can be.

In order to illuminate the role of self- and peer-assessment in practice, this book also contains seven bioscience case studies. Expanded versions of these and other case studies, marking criteria, and video streams of peer-assessment in action, are available from the website supporting this guide (http://www.bioscience.heacademy.ac.uk/ TeachingGuides/). In addition, the chapters draw on a number of specific examples from published research of practice, each chosen because they illustrate a particular aspect of the assessment process well. Whilst some of these examples are from bioscience, a number are not, but in these cases the examples can be readily transferred into a biosciences setting.

TABLE 1. A COMPARISON BETWEEN SELF- AND PEER-ASSESSMENT AND OTHER ASSESSMENTS

Self- and Peer-Assessment	Other Assessments
Student-centred.	Students often excluded.
Clear transparent criteria.	Norm referenced assessment. Or if criteria used, these may be given to students without discussion.
Student empowered. There is a strong sense of personal ownership.	Students isolated from the assessment and therefore from the learning process.
Likely to encourage a deep approach to learning.	Likely to foster a surface approach to learning.
Allows students to actively construct their learning.	Does not provide the incentives to construct own learning.
Encourages discussion between students and tutors.	Little discussion, sometimes none.
Formative feedback.	Feedback misunderstandings due to lapse of time or loss of ongoing communication between student and tutor.
Opportunity to revise or review weak areas of learning.	Results final, with little point in going back over boxes 'ticked'.
More trial and less error in student learning.	Results received too late in the method to revisit or be useful in learning process. Little trial and a lot of error in learning.
Prepares students for the lifelong ongoing journey of learning.	Often end-point destination only learning.
For peer-assessment often several assessors.	One assessor and a moderator or at most two assessors.
Provides good opportunities for formative assessment.	Little formative assessment.
Likely to increases student's confidence.	Limited or negative effect on confidence.
Increased performance/learning quality of the learning output.	–
Often authentic learning tasks.	Rarely authentic learning tasks.

INVOLVING STUDENTS IN ASSESSMENT

A CONSIDERATION OF CURRENT ASSESSMENT PRACTICE IN HIGHER EDUCATION

The reason why it is desirable and infinitely sensible to have students involved and central to the assessment process is well illustrated by Boud and Falchikov (1989), 'teachers have limited access to the knowledge of their students and in many ways students have greater insights into their own achievements'. The fact that this is not normally recognised in higher education is a serious concern, as reflected by Boud (1995) 'there is probably more bad practice and ignorance of significant issues in the area of assessment than in any other aspect of higher education. Assessment acts as a mechanism to control students that is far more pervasive and insidious than most staff would be prepared to acknowledge'. This is unfortunate, as assessment is a foundation of student achievement and therefore regarded as a measure of institutional success. Why, if assessment is so important to undergraduate learning experiences, should bad practice exist?

There may be a number of reasons for a lack of student involvement. Increasingly in higher education, there is greater cross-disciplinary teaching taking place. Courses like forensic science involve tutors from different departments such as biology, chemistry and law, and each department may have their 'own' understanding of assessment within their own structure of assessment policies. Institutions may also be presenting tutors with too many assessment options without looking into or understanding them fully. In a recent publication, Knight (2001) presented fifty assessment techniques. For some, this diversity may be heaven sent, but for others it could be thoroughly overwhelming; and without guidance, many excellent tutors can be left not knowing where to begin.

Because of this mix of practice, assessment processes in higher education generate a mixture of concerns, such as:

Criteria concerns

- 'Norm' referenced marking; grading students according to how they compare against each other as a class. Norm referencing may still be the 'naturally' preferred model of assessment by most markers, Rust *et al.* (2003).

- Criteria referenced marking, where grading is expressed according to each student's performance, may have criteria and individual weightings that are often unclear and not constructed with the involvement of students.

Assessment deficiencies

- Learners ill-informed about what they need to know in order to understand or do. Interestingly, Gabb (1981) reported that the only piece of assessment information given to a cohort of students preparing to undertake final year projects was the name of the assessor. In response to this limited information, students deduced and developed their own sets of assessment rules, by which they tried to work out how best to pass the assessment.

- The development of a truly hidden and non-transparent curriculum, described by Sambell and McDowell (1998) as 'the shadowy, ill-defined and amorphous nature of that which is implicit and embedded in educational experiences in contrast with formal statements about curricula and the surface features of educational interaction.'

Tutor folklore

- Community discussions between academics in a field developed through years of experience, concerning assessing and teaching (Edwards and Knight, 1995).

Feedback concerns

- Feedback can be given too late to be of benefit.

- Feedback can be diminished in usefulness because students do not understand it or perceive its importance (Chanock, 2000).

Traditionally, so-called 'summative' assessment, (for example, end of module examinations), has been used to determine how much 'learning' has taken place. Used here, summative refers to an end-point mark, which influences student progression and may contribute towards their degree classification. Failing an assessment may mean students do not progress, yet passing does not always indicate meaningful learning, as demonstrated by these student interview quotes from Brown *et al.* (1998); 'you shallow learn for an exam but you don't know the stuff. It's poor learning which you quickly forget', and 'you think just let me remember this for the next hour and a half. Then you don't care'. These students appear to see learning as an end product of assessment and view the learning quantitatively, which means that to be a good learner is to know more. The student learning which higher education needs to encourage is qualitative learning, where new material can be interpreted and incorporated, so that understanding is progressively changed through an ongoing, updating process (Biggs, 1996).

Underpinning many existing assessment processes is the issue of ownership and hence power. When referring to the goal of education, Rogers (2003) made the distinction between authoritarian or democratic philosophies. Heron (1992) distinguished authority in education as being either benign, luminous and truly educative, or punitive, indoctrinating and intimidating. It is the latter which formed the basis for his authoritarian model (so called because of the unilateral control of assessment by staff). For Heron (1988), power lay with those who make decisions about other people. Students are considered rationally competent to grasp a major discipline, but perversely are not considered competent to engage with the educational decision-making, whereby this grasp may be fully achieved. If, as Heron believed, the objective of the process of education is the emergence of a self-determining person, i.e. someone who can set their own learning objectives

(outcomes), devise a rational programme to attain them, set criteria of excellence by which work is assessed and assess their own work, then the 'unilateral control and assessment of students by staff means that the process of education is at odds with the objective of that process' (Heron, 1988).

A NEED FOR CHANGE IN ASSESSMENT PRACTICE

Sixteen years ago, Heron (1988) thought the time was ripe for an educational change from the authoritarian model to one which is student inclusive. Almost ten years after Heron's call for change, came the publication of *Higher Education in the Learning Society*. The Dearing Report (1997), as it became known, perhaps noting that little, or no change had occurred, attempted to prime teaching staff in universities to make a professional commitment to teaching. Dearing addressed as a priority the improvement of the student learning environments, recommended that learning and teaching strategies should now focus on the promotion of student learning and stressed that a radical change to teaching was needed.

The impact of Dearing on assessment may be gauged by the comments of Brown and Glasner (2003), who noted that the range of ways in which students are assessed is unfortunately extremely limited with around 80 per cent of assessment being in the form of exams, essays or reports of some kind. This may only partly reflect what is assessed, consisting of a very limited range of student skills, knowledge and ability. Students appear to do the same old types of activities again and again. It may have been as a result of these same old activities that Boud (2000) was led to assert that 'assessment practices in higher education institutions tend not to equip students well for the process of effective learning in a learning society'. Boud's comments shed further light on the impact of the Dearing report, as the use of the 'learning society' formed part of its title. Dearing's view of the learning society reflected a 'vision' of a society (individuals, the state, employers and providers of education and training) committed to learning throughout life, more as a process or journey of discovery, rather than a ticked box outcome. Boud (2000) discussed a more complex view of the learning society in which 'those who are skilled and flexible learners will flourish, others will languish'. Thus a need for change within assessment is evident to encourage progressive learning, as skilled and flexible learners are unlikely products of Heron's authoritarian model of assessment. The way forward is to look for a model of student assessment which is inclusive, involving students and tutors working collaboratively. Self- and peer-assessments provide just that model.

SELF- AND PEER-ASSESSMENT: A WAY TO IMPLEMENT CHANGE

Writing in the early 1950s, Rogers (2003) outlined the goals of democratic education, in assisting students to become individuals. He included such attributes as being 'a critical learner, able to evaluate the contributions made by others and being able to self-initiate actions and be responsible for those actions'. Furthermore, he went on to say that, 'we cannot teach another person directly; we can only facilitate their learning. A person learns significantly only those things which they perceive as being involved in the maintenance of, or enhancement of, the structure of self'. These are sentiments which underly self- and peer-assessment philosophy. The defining characteristic of self-assessment is the 'involvement of students in identifying standards and/or criteria to apply to their work and making judgements about the extent to which they have met these criteria and standards' (Boud, 1986). Peer-assessment has been defined (Topping *et al.*, 2000) as 'an arrangement for peers to consider the level, value, worth, quality or successfulness of the products or outcomes of learning of others of similar status'. From these definitions it becomes apparent that self- and peer-assessments are not methods of assessment but sources of assessment that may be used within a framework of different methods (Brown *et al.*, 1997).

At the heart of both of these assessment processes is the student. Brew (1995) commenting on the conceptual shift in higher education from a focus on teaching, to a perspective in which student learning is central, illustrates the importance of this student centredness, 'the essence of the learning perspective is that it considers all decisions about teaching and assessment in the light of the impact or potential impact on student learning'. Both self- and peer-assessment appear to have an emphasis on developing student autonomy, which, while not an easy concept to define, does have 'some of the attributes required by anyone if they are to be effective learners'. After all, being dependent on others (teachers) and not being able to plan and manage your own journey, or process of lifelong learning will not be effective preparation for learning and the world of employment (Boud, 1988).

The model shown in Figure 1 from Higgs (1988) is of autonomous learning. It shows how the four principal elements of learner, teacher, task and environment interact together. How successful the interaction is, depends mainly on the extent to which the elements are consistent with each other and upon certain specific assumptions, such as, that self-directed learning needs to be active and not passive. More importantly, the outcomes of learning are

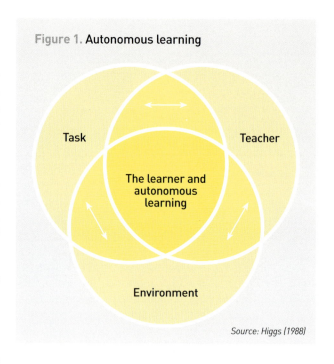

Figure 1. Autonomous learning

Source: Higgs (1988)

dependent on the assessment process. In the self-determining student who will be self-assessing, the assessment will be included in the process of learning, as well as work done on the content of the learning. Therefore assessing how learning takes place and considering how evidence is provided of what has been learnt is fundamentally more important than assessing what has been learnt or memorized. The shift to self-determination and self-assessment starts to make the process more important than content (Heron, 1988). Some may consider that Heron demotes content too much, believing, with some justification, that a balance needs to be established between the process of learning and the content of learning. However, the stress on the process and the content in self- and peer-assessment highlights the need for effective communication between students and tutors concerning the use of appropriate tasks and activities. This is well illustrated, for example, in the need for tutor and student to discuss and agree assessment criteria, which results in students having a greater degree of ownership of each assessment they are undertaking (Falchikov and Boud, 1989). While it is evident that greater ownership may also be related to a shift in power, a note of caution needs to be expressed. Tan (2004) argues that while self-assessment provides students 'with more autonomy to judge their own work, more is known about the students in terms of how they view themselves'. This has implications for how power is manifested within the assessment process. Therefore, it is vital for student empowerment to understand the ways in which power is exercised.

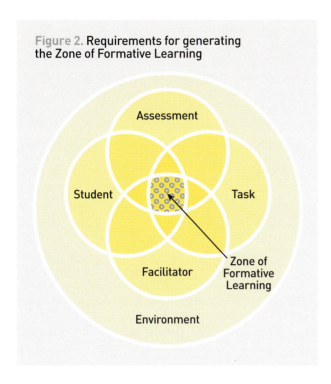

Figure 2. **Requirements for generating the Zone of Formative Learning**

Assessment

Student

Task

Facilitator

Zone of Formative Learning

Environment

With this increased ownership, it may be possible to reconsider Figure 1 to explicitly include assessment. In Figure 2, the environment provides the overall background in which the learning occurs. The environment is formed from a number of things such as, the learning and teaching beliefs of departments or faculties, as well as, the human and physical resource issues. The environment influences in varying ways the student, the facilitator, the assessment practice and the assessment task(s). These four separate components all overlap at a given focus, becoming one. It is here that students' learning is shaped; this is the Zone of Formative Learning. Assessment is, therefore, inclusive in the learning process.

Hinett (1995) in a study which compared assessment practice at a British University with that carried out at the Alverno College Milwaukee USA reported how effectively this close integration can work at an institutional level. A major difference in the approach to assessment was in the use of self- and peer-assessment. At Alverno; each student was actively encouraged to self- and peer-assess. Attitudes ranged from 'it's painful, but it works and I learn more' to 'I like self-assessment because I can reflect back and know I should study more in this area'.

At the British University little value was given to self- and peer-assessment, which meant students lacked confidence and faith in their own judgements. On self-assessment, some typical comments students made were that 'no-one takes it seriously' and 'it is just a hassle'. Furthermore, students learnt in a prescriptive environment, being told 'you will do this'. They generally validated their work in terms of

grades and admitted to getting into the mentality of 'what am I going to get out of this in terms of credit'. When asked 'How do you know what is expected of you?', the majority suggested that they didn't really know as 'they never actually say what they are looking for'. Students also often talked of 'guessing'.

Students at Alverno used feedback constructively, to help them to plan their work and to understand how they were developing as learners. Explicit criteria and learning integrated with the assessment process allowed students, through self-assessment, to take control of their own learning.

Before considering self- and peer-assessment in a little more detail, it would help to be familiar with some aspects of the learning process.

THEORETICAL FRAMEWORKS TO LEARNING

Falchikov (2001) observed that 'too many educational initiatives appear to be devoid of theoretical underpinning, seeming to be driven by expediency, economics or political agendas'. Perhaps educational initiatives will go on being at least influenced by such as factors. However, learning through self- and peer-assessment can only be understood within a theoretical learning framework. There are two influential theories of learning that we need consider.

Piaget and learning

Piaget believed that each child passed through a series of stages of thinking which were qualitatively different from each other (Sutherland, 1992). A child actively constructs their knowledge of the world around them as a result of various encounters with the environment, and also, by, communicating with other children, as discussion can challenge existing schemes or concepts leading to a re-think of an original point of view. In this way the child learns by a series of adjustments to their environment, which is achieved through using two alternative mechanisms within the process — assimilation and accommodation — which are balanced through equilibration. In this way, new material being assimilated by the learner can be modified against previous concepts, which are stored in the memory as learning progresses. These individual pieces of information are themselves up-dated by the mechanism of accommodation and transformed into new material and a more complete understanding. Piaget's views of learning are of particular importance to those of us in education in a number of rather significant ways. For example, they underpin the learning cycle proposed by Kolb, which has prominence in higher education as a model to aid understanding the learning process. Kolb's learning cycle has frequently been reinterpreted

Figure 3. Structural dimensions underlying the process of experiential learning and the resulting basic knowledge forms

Source: Kolb (1984)

and is often presented in a very simplified form. In Figure 3, the unabridged learning cycle (Kolb, 1984), with its strong reference to Piaget's work is illustrated. Looking at the cycle, we can see it represents a very personal cycle of learning, self-contained from outside social and professional influences. The learner is very reliant on their own perceptions of their learning experience.

Vygotsky and learning

Like Piaget, Vygotsky (1978) believed that children constructed their own learning. Vygotsky was aware that children, often unable to perform tasks or solve problems alone often succeeded when an adult helped them. Piaget took a dim view of success obtained in this way, claiming that it involved the teaching and learning of procedures and not the development of fully integrated learning and understanding. For Piaget, genuine intellectual competence was a manifestation of a child's largely unassisted activities (Wood, 1988), whereas Vygotsky saw intervention as important. 'The difference between twelve and eight, or between nine and eight is what we call the Zone of Proximal Development (ZPD). It is the distance between the actual developmental level as determined by independent problem solving, and the level of potential development as determined through problem solving under adult guidance or in collaboration with a more capable peer' Vygotsky (1978).

For Vygotsky, 'learning awakens a variety of internal developmental processes that are able to

operate only when the child is interacting with other people in his environment and in cooperation with his peers. Once these processes are fully internalised they become part of the child's independent development achievement'. Therefore, while both Piaget and Vygotsky placed a very strong emphasis on activity as the basis for learning, Vygotsky emphasised communication and social interaction, where teachers (either adults or more experienced peers) retain varying degrees of influence over each child's learning activities. Wood *et al.*, (1976) saw the intervention of a tutor as involving a kind of 'scaffolding' process that enables a child or novice to solve a problem or achieve a goal which would be beyond his or her unassisted efforts.

The theoretical underpinnings of the work of Piaget and Vygotsky are recognisably used in higher education today with regards to self- and peer-assessment. Peer-assessment is grounded in philosophies of active learning, and may be seen as being a manifestation of social construction, because it involves the joint construction of knowledge through discourse (Falchikov and Goldfinch, 2000). Falchikov (2001) draws our attention to both the work of Piaget and Vygotsky with respect to peer tutoring, and emphasises the role of self- and peer-assessment in peer tutoring. One of the arguments used by Falchikov (2003) to illustrate that self- and peer-assessment are for educational and not just training purposes is that Piagetian theory stresses the importance of practical concrete experiences for cognitive development. The role of experience, with social and cultural influences in learning, is very relevant to self-assessment (Brew 1995). MacDonald (2004) discussed the practical implications of implementing online pedagogies and stressed the communicative potential of e-learning employing a social constructivist approach. It has already been seen how Piagetian thinking is compatible with Kolb's learning cycle; but Kolb (1984) also appears to draw on a Vygotsky social constructivism. This, a less discussed aspect of the Kolb learning cycle, is of immense importance in relation to self- and peer-assessment.

APPROACHES TO LEARNING

Deep and surface approaches

A number of advocates of self-assessment relate approaches to learning as so-called 'deep' and 'surface'. Marton and Saljo (1976) explored the processes and strategies of learning used by students as well as the outcomes of that learning, in terms of what is understood and remembered. They found two different levels of processing which they called deep-level and surface-level processing. 'In the case of surface-level processing, each student directed his attention towards learning text itself (the sign), i.e. he had a reproductive conception of learning which meant that he was more or less forced to keep to a rote-learning strategy. In the case of deep-level processing, the student was directed towards the intentional context of the learning material (what was signified), i.e. he was directed towards comprehending what the author wanted to say about a certain scientific problem or principle' (Marton and Saljo, 1976). Students are not necessarily deep or surface learners, but they can take a deep or surface approach to learning depending on the circumstances. For example, someone might normally adopt a deep approach to a subject, but under pressure of an impending examination they might switch to a surface approach (Brew, 1995).

SUMMARY

Students are central in both self- and peer-assessment. As such, both sources of assessment can be used to enthuse, enable and empower students within a variety of assessment methods. The evidence for the type and approaches to learning encouraged by self- and peer-assessments is theoretically strong, with an emphasis on students constructing knowledge within a formative learning environment. With self- and peer-assessment, learning is more fully integrated with assessment, and not just a by-product of assessment. Ideally, students should grow in the use of self- and peer-assessment throughout their university experience, because the ultimate goals, successful and meaningful learning, are essential in preparation for the learning society.

2

GETTING STARTED
WITH SELF- AND PEER-ASSESSMENT

ASSESSMENT CRITERIA

Definition and rationale

The role of the criteria is fundamental to self- and peer-assessment because criteria provide an objective structure for those who generate and implement them. Marking criteria are, in effect, the seat of ownership. Sadler (1989) defines a criterion as 'a distinguishing property or characteristic of any thing, by which its quality can be judged or estimated, or by which a decision or classification may be made'. Without criteria, academics rely covertly on an expert's notion of quality. There is a connoisseurship; judges 'know' what the standards are and how to use them (Sadler, 1989). There is a reliance on tacit assessment knowledge, knowledge regarding assessment that is in the head of the tutor and not necessarily made explicit to students (or other tutors). This approach to marking is not acceptable for the reasons already considered in Chapter 1, primarily, the exclusion of students from the assessment process. Furthermore, Ecclestone (2001) illustrates other considerations for using criteria such as enhanced reliability, as criteria make assessment more amenable to moderation and standardisation.

Self- and peer- assessment: introducing the criteria

Students are often unfamiliar with marking criteria. Hence, they need to be clearly introduced to them at the beginning of their course of study. Boud (1986) considered primarily self-assessment, but made suggestions which are also applicable to peer-assessment. In order to try to resolve the issue of criteria, students and staff should attempt to clarify the concepts of assessment criteria. Where possible, tutors should not impose, but listen to the student's perception of the criteria. Joint discussion may help avoid any mismatch in interpretation of the criteria or an individual criterion (Orsmond *et al.*, 1996, 1997 and 2000). Further discussion regarding interpretation of the criteria can be found in Case Study 1 (Merry and Orsmond) at the back of this guide. Rust *et al.*, (2003) also investigated student understanding of assessment criteria and the assessment process. They too found a mismatch of interpretation with difficult criteria, such as analysis and evaluation.

Discussions may initially take the form of asking:

'What would be the factors which characterised a good assignment on this course?'

Once this process has been completed, the elements of satisfactory criteria should be considered. This entails such information as:

- the area to be assessed;

- the aims of the assessment;

- the standards to be reached.

Generating assessment criteria

Boud (1986) highlighted the importance of students reaching their own decisions about the criteria for assessing themselves but stressed the facilitative role the teacher plays in this process. Two techniques for facilitating understanding of criteria are considered:

1. Structured written schedules for developing individual criteria

2. Structured group activities for reaching consensus on common criteria

1. Structured written schedules
These provide a list of instructions guiding students through a sequence of steps involving:

- identifying the criteria, which they consider appropriate to apply to their work;

- clarifying these criteria;

- assessing the priority, or emphasis, which they wish to give to each criterion.

Working with students who have perhaps started a task or who are more experienced in self- and peer-assessment might require different types of questions. Brown *et al.,* (1997) gave some suggestions, such as:

- what do I think about what I have been doing?

- how could I improve my approach?

Once satisfactory criteria have been generated in this way, students use them as a yardstick by which they are able to judge their own performance. This might involve:

- awarding themselves a mark with respect to each criterion; and then

- making a statement justifying that mark.

2. Structured group activities
Boud (1986) suggested structured group activities if common criteria for a class are required. This will involve the group (groups) identifying, discussing and agreeing upon a common set of criteria. Initially students are briefed that they will be expected to produce a number of criteria. There then follow a number of sessions where criteria are clarified and discussed.
Freeman and Lewis (1998) also provided suggestions for group construction of criteria. These suggestions particularly lend themselves to engaging students with self- or peer-assessment by asking them to consider some of their own existing course-work, perhaps with the accompanying feedback:

- ask students to review their returned assignment in pairs or as individuals;

- ask them to make brief notes, concerning where they gained or lost marks;

- from these notes draw up a list of the criteria students thought the tutor seemed to be using. These criteria can be discussed further for greater clarity.

By viewing student learning as a journey, the ongoing or re-evaluating of the initial joint discussion regarding criteria is necessary to support the learning that the students are undertaking. This can be seen as a first stage in the self- and peer-assessment process.
The above suggestions are helpful, but some care needs to be taken. For example, students who undertake a poster assignment in a level one microbiology session may also be undertaking a poster assignment in level one physiology. The students may think that the end product of the assessment is 'making a poster'. However, the purpose of the assessed assignment may be the demonstration of specific learning outcomes through a poster, not the making of the poster *per se*. So students need to be clear that the physiology assignment requires demonstration of certain processing outcomes, which may, or may not, be very different from those outcomes demonstrated through the creation of their microbiology posters.
The more experienced students become, the more their approach to criteria construction changes. Sivan, (2000) illustrated this well when discussing how students with previous experience of peer-assessment approached criteria construction. Students were seen to take 'a further step and initiated the allocation of different weighting to each criterion and thus were taking even more responsibility for their own learning'. This acceptance of responsibility further develops a student's sense of 'ownership' of the assessment process and further strengthens a student's claim of being an autonomous learner.
The practise and understanding of self- and peer-assessment develops through use as a course or as education progresses, leading to a deeper understanding of the assessment and criteria requirements as the learning journey progresses.

Self- and peer-assessment: criteria implementation
Different types of criteria can be used to generate different forms of judgements. Miller (2003) considered the implementation of criteria within a self- and peer-assessment context. Miller, looking at oral presentation over two consecutive years, wanted to change assessment marking from looking at a few global components of performance such as clarity

and interaction, (used in 2000) to multiple, very discrete components of performance such as 'the presentation included a plan for community and/or work re-integration' (used in 2001). The reason for this shift was to tackle the tendency for markers to assign scores in a very narrow range, concentrating at the high end of the scoring scale. The results indicated that:

- the initial assessment sheet with questions elicited greater feedback from the markers;

- the revised assessment sheet elicited fewer comments and a larger percentage of negative feedback.

Miller explained this result as a consequence of markers being more critically analytical of the presentation when using the revised sheet. However, it could be that, with a set of discrete statements, there was less the students were unclear about, or perhaps the students did not fully understand the statements, and so were unable to structure questions as well. Furthermore, the use of statements may prove limiting or even detrimental to the learning process. This could occur in a number of ways. Firstly, this form of listed 'closed' statements in an assessment sheet may be less than inspiring to students, as the statements could, even if very carefully worded, be based upon the tutor's singular, and perhaps biased, view of what may, or may not, have occurred. Secondly, rather than help students focus on their own personal learning experiences, statements may, instead, severely limit free and honest individual expression from the student, which would then be detrimental to both students and tutors throughout the course, thereby unwittingly limiting the students' learning potential.

Ultimately, Miller (2003) made an important statement, the highly specific assessment instrument, as opposed to the more global instrument, 'produces better quantitative differentiation of levels of performance at the expense of losing qualitative feedback'. It is very important to be aware before implementing specific types of criteria, what exactly you are hoping to achieve with them. Using Miller's example above, are you looking for the 'quantitative' or 'qualitative'? Knowing this not only lends credibility to the assessment process, but provides useful information, particularly for evaluation purposes.

There are some situations where tutors do not always have total control over how a module runs. Tutors are increasingly finding themselves 'team teaching' where the criteria are defined, perhaps by one person, but implemented by the whole team. Tutors, particularly in the case of new tutors, may find

themselves taking over a module where the criteria are already defined. Often in such situations tutors cannot involve students in construction of the criteria, but that does not necessarily mean that students need be excluded from working with those criteria. There are things that can be done. Here is an example:

- Take the marking criteria and consider the terms used to define the aspects of the assignment to be assessed. One example would be if looking into experimental design then part of the criteria may be to consider how 'robust' and 'rigorous' the design is.

- Make a list of the criteria terms used.

- Ask the students to write down their definitions of each term.

- Collect in the definitions, read them and note the correct ones for each term and the other definitions used. This second part is important, because incorrect definitions may give you an insight into student thinking and highlight any common misconceptions.

- Feedback to the students the range of definition they have used, indicating the ones which are correct.

This is not ideal, but at least students do have involvement in the criteria, and furthermore the ground has now been prepared for further discussions, perhaps in subsequent tutorials. Tutorial work is useful for discussing assessment issues. Adams and King (1995) using six tutorial groups engaged students with self-assessment in a class of 120. Race (1998) outlines a process list for peer-assessment which can be used for groups of up to 100 and takes less than an hour to implement.

Self- and peer-assessment: using marking criteria to help in making judgements

Making judgements is ultimately what assessment is all about. Having explicit and unambiguous criteria helps this process, but it is still a challenge for students to take their own work and make judgements about it. Peers can be useful in helping students develop their ability to judge. 'While peers may be unwilling to make formal assessment of their peers they may be more positive when students have to give specific feedback of a descriptive nature for the benefit of their peers and no grading has taken place' (Boud, 1986). When using criteria, remember they are reference points in the process of judgement, aids not replacements (Knight and Yorke, 2003).

Making judgements does not, then, simply involve marking work. Peer review is a helpful way to approach peer-assessment (Pond *et al.*, 1995). When asking students to make judgements about their own work or that of their peers, it is important to consider time pressures. For guidance, if considering poster work, students can provide useful written feedback (with or without a mark), on approximately three or four pieces of work in an hour (depending on their complexity).

Elwood and Klenowski (2002) offered students structured support which considered criteria development and help in making judgements about their work, which incorporates a modelling process which considered six separate topics such as, demonstration of understanding of criteria by grading an assignment.

Computer-based programmes are increasingly being used for assessment purposes. The Many Using and Creative Hypermedia system (MUCH) is a multi-user hypermedia tool that supports collaborative learning and has proved to be suitable for peer-assessment (Rushton *et al.*, 1993). Another computer system called 'Peers' has been successfully used to undertake peer-assessment allowing staff and students to determine criteria and weightings for each criterion (Ngu *et al.*, 1995). The case study (Case Study 2) provided by Kuri stresses two strengths of peer-assessment with respect to criteria, empowerment and peer use of feedback. The use of online learning often allows detailed and personalised feedback to be exchanged quickly thus enhancing its potential effectiveness.

Time does need to be allocated to help students in making judgements using criteria as these comments from a study by Brown *et al.*, (1998) illustrate:

'Grading is really hard, to know whether to give them a 2 or a 4, I've know idea how you draw the line, I just know if someone is good or not'.

'I sat there with these numbers and in the end it became a bit random. Perhaps the tutor finds it easier to break it all down into a section, that's up to her. But I just get a general feeling that's all.'

However, the more students undertake exercises involving generating and applying criteria, the more comfortable they become. A quote from a study interview sums this up well:

'When I did it the first time, I need longer to think what grade I should give to this group. Besides, I worried a lot whether I gave a fair mark to others. However, I can do it quite fast this time ... More you do, better you can do it' (Sivan 2000).

Using criteria and making judgements in a meaningful way does not just happen after one attempt, students need practice to develop the abilities required. Because of this, it is important that, teaching tutors, try their best to get self- and peer-assessment practices implemented at an early stage within a student's university career, and provide a progression of self- and peer-activities throughout a student's university course of studies. Adams and King (1995) give an indication how this could be done. Sluijsman, (2002) presents a framework with guidance on how to realise integrated peer-assessment activities.

However, a note of caution: just because you have worked through a criteria construction process with students, this is no guarantee that all your students will necessarily understand it. Many will, but some may not. The more experienced students become in working with criteria, the fewer the problems of misunderstanding. However, as with any assessment practice some students may misunderstand.

Lack of understanding may be only one cause of disagreements. Hughes and Large (1993) discuss variability in the marking of oral presentation in pharmacology students despite working with agreed marking criteria. They identify issues separate from the criteria such as, how the 'voice' of the speaker may be heard by those near the front of the lecture theatre and inaudible at the back; or how overhead transparencies may be readable at close quarters but unreadable from a distance.

ASSESSMENT: VALIDITY AND RELIABILITY

Only a valid and reliable assessment processes should be used to determine what learning has occurred. Reliability of assessment is defined by Fry *et al.*, (1999) as 'the assessment process would generate the same results if repeated on another occasion with the same group, or if repeated with another group of similar students'. Validity is defined as 'adequacy and appropriateness of the task/test in relation to the outcomes/objectives of the teaching being assessed', i.e. it measures what it is supposed to measure. These general definitions have been developed; for example, Gielen *et al.*, (2003) consider the validity of assessment scoring, and whether scores are valid. In this respect the criterion of fairness plays an important role.

Self- assessment: validity and reliability

Three studies which consider validity and reliability have implications for implementing and evaluating self-assessment. Boud and Falchikov (1989) reviewed 48 studies of student self-ratings compared to the ratings of students by teachers. Some of the outcomes were:

- comparing results from a number of studies showed that there is no consistent tendency to over or underestimate performance;

- when asked to rate themselves on a marking scale, able and mature students are able to do so. Able students when new to a subject are aware of, and concentrate on, their own deficiencies, and thus underrate their work.

Falchikov and Boud (1989) undertook a meta-analysis of 57 quantitative self-assessment studies used in higher education. Some of the outcomes were:

- the role of seniority or duration of enrolment of the marker was found to be less important than expertise in a given subject;

- explicit criteria led to greater accuracy of rating as did criteria that students felt they owned when compared to criteria that were provided;

- better-designed study was associated with a closer correspondence between student and tutor compared to poorly designed studies.

Boud (1989) raised the question, 'if there is a high correlation between marks generated by students and those generated by staff, why bother with involving students if their contribution makes no difference to the final grade?' He provided two suggestions:

- self-assessment provides practice in the interpretation of the often arbitrary require-ments which most public work needs to satisfy.

- expediency: if students can take a greater role in assessment there is the potential for the saving of staff time on the often tedious task of marking.

Regardless of the correlation between marks, considering marks themselves as an important indicator may be missing the point. Topping (2003) comments 'that the high correlation between measures is in any event redundant, and the processes here are at least as important as the actual judgements'. Engage-ment in self-assessment is a good way to improve performance and nudge students forward in their Zones of Proximal Development. The case study by Rushton (Case Study 3) at the back of this guide stresses the learning that takes place as a result of self- or peer-assessment.

Peer-assessment: validity and reliability

Falchikov and Goldfinch (2000) carried out a meta-analysis comparing peer-assessed and teacher marks.

This study can be seen as a companion piece to the paper by Falchikov and Boud (1989). Some of the outcomes of this peer-assessment study were similar to the outcome for the self-assessment study:

- high-quality studies were associated with better peer-faculty agreement than studies of lower quality;

- student familiarity with the ownership of criteria tended to enhance peer-assessment validity.

However, there were differences compared to the self-assessment study:

- Unlike self-assessment where the level of the course appeared to be a salient variable, peer-assessment does not seem to be less valid in lower-level courses. A possible explanation is that participants in peer-assessment studies are, in general, well prepared.

- There was no clear subject area difference.

Finally, some areas were measured in peer-assessments that were not considered in self-assess-ment. Peer marking of several individual dimensions appeared less valid than peer-assessment that required global judgement, based on well-defined and well-understood criteria.

A number of concerns, which have implications for the implementation and evaluation of self- and peer-assessment, have been expressed concerning bias in peer-assessment. Magin (1993), accepting the criticism, where a peer mark is based on an individual peer rating, described a study where multiple ratings are used. The effect of a lenient or severe mark is diluted by the marks from the other students. An interesting approach to dealing with lenient or harsh markers is reported in the case study by Cogdell *et al.*, (Case Study 4 at the back of this guide). In another study, Magin (2001) studied the relational 'reciprocity' effect of peer-assessment of group work. Only 1 per cent of the variance in peer scores was due to bias. In considering gender bias, Falchikov and Magin (1997) used a system that considered student ratings from same and opposite sex, found marginal differences favouring females in peer-assessment.

A brief but useful and in-depth review of validity and reliability in self- and peer-assessment exists (Topping, 2003). Within bioscience, Stefani (1994) found student assessment to be as reliable as that of lecturers, and also reflected on the power/ownership debate, advocating the early introduction in the students' careers of self- and peer-assessment for summative and formative assessment.

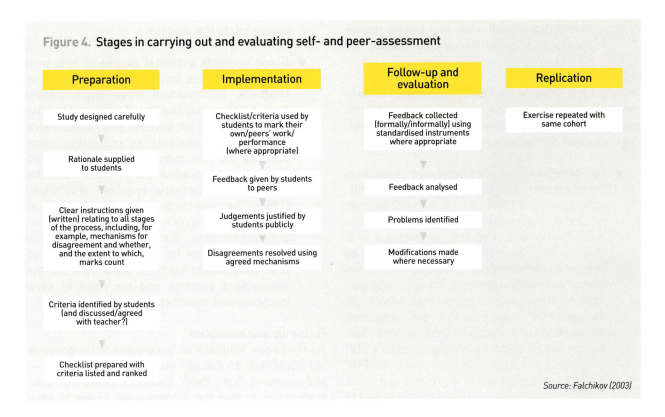

Figure 4. Stages in carrying out and evaluating self- and peer-assessment

Preparation	Implementation	Follow-up and evaluation	Replication
Study designed carefully	Checklist/criteria used by students to mark their own/peers' work/ performance (where appropriate)	Feedback collected (formally/informally) using standardised instruments where appropriate	Exercise repeated with same cohort
Rationale supplied to students	Feedback given by students to peers	Feedback analysed	
Clear instructions given (written) relating to all stages of the process, including, for example, mechanisms for disagreement and whether, and the extent to which, marks count	Judgements justified by students publicly	Problems identified	
	Disagreements resolved using agreed mechanisms	Modifications made where necessary	
Criteria identified by students (and discussed/agreed with teacher?)			
Checklist prepared with criteria listed and ranked			

Source: Falchikov (2003)

SELF- AND PEER-ASSESSMENT: HOW IS IT CARRIED OUT AND EVALUATED?

Developing and implementing the marking criteria are major parts of carrying out self- and peer-assessment. However, there are a number of stages that need planning when carrying out and evaluating self- and peer-assessment. These have been documented (Falchikov 2003). Figure 4 is taken from this work. While this diagram is in some ways self explanatory and a number of issues have been covered already, a little commentary may clarify and refine.

Preparation

- Remember the principles of good experimental design. In order to evaluate the procedure subsequently, the dependant variables need to be identified, such as the agreement between peers and tutor, or a measure of the benefits to learning experienced by the participants (Falchikov 2003).

- Students need to be well briefed in advance of the assessment practice and this may mean including details in module/award handbooks, which are often written months in advance of teaching.

- Information should be given both in writing and verbally. Try to ensure that students see and are familiar with the use of all documents, such as evaluation forms, and have the opportunity to question, clarify and check all material.

- Most importantly, clearly articulate the rationale for using self- and/or peer-assessment. This may make planning the assessment more meaningful. If students have motivation, they are more likely to engage in the assessment task. For example, if the reason is primarily to engage students in the assessment process *per se,* then you will plan differently than if the reason was to make students aware of how to use feedback through peer- or self-formative assessment. Often this is a case of emphasis and the focus of the task.

- Particularly with students new to the process, discuss issues related to fairness and bias (Sivan, 2000).

- Have an effectively detailed approach as to how self- or peer-assessment is to be 'policed' and 'controlled'. Assessment criteria can help with the marking, but some students may under- or over-mark. You need to talk to the students about the consequences of this type of marking (Adams and King, 1995). Race (1998) has some suggestions on how this may be done which include, moderation of peer marking, monitoring student achievement and providing mark-free rehearsal opportunities. Moderation of marks is a difficult issue as it closely relates to the issues of power discussed in Chapter 1.

Implementation

Perhaps here it may be appropriate to consider when to use self-assessment, when to use peer-assessment, and when to use both. There are no clear rules. However, there are some things you may wish to consider:

- Self-assessment is not undertaken in isolation from others. 'The defining feature of self-assessment is that the individual learner ultimately makes a judgement about what has been learnt, not that others have no input to it' Boud (1995). So, self-assessment should be seen as a continual process, used by students as part of their natural learning. It may initially lend itself to some exercise rather than others, for example PDP. The initials PDP are sometimes assumed to mean Personal Development Plan, but the last P indicates planning. Therefore PDP is a process carried out over time. In PDP students are often asked to reflect and write about those reflections. This is ideally suited to self-assessment or self-evaluation processes. (The distinction between assessment and evaluation is discussed in Chapter 3).

- Sometimes you may wish to use student-centred assessment practices for semi-pragmatic reasons. The case study by Hughes (Case Study 5) illustrates this well. Here peer-assessment is used to reduce marking time, but also provides a range of benefits for students.

- Race (1998) lists a range of activities where peer-assessment can be used, such as in student presentation, interviews and practical work. Peer-assessment also lends itself to group work and there are a number of examples of this (Cheng and Warren, 1999; Freeman, 1995; Goldfinch, 1994; Li, 2001 and Lekj and Wyvill, 2002).

- Assessment practices should relate to the learning outcomes to be achieved. Therefore, check what the outcomes say as this may give guidance as to which student-centred practice to use.

- Boud (1986) gave guidance on giving and receiving feedback. It is a key area and students will need some preparation in matters such as resolving disagreements. To faciliate students in their learning, it is best to introduce guidance early, rather than just before the assessed product is produced, to allow time for students to assimilate the process.

- Giving students a greater degree of help with marking, and also focusing on the provision of feedback, is important when implementing peer-assessment. The Peer Feedback Marking (PFM) designed to develop peer-assessment was rated by students as conferring more benefits than the more usual lecture marked methods. It also enhanced reflection and the delivery of diplomatic criticism (Falchikov, (1995). The case study by Reed (Case Study 6) gives an indication of how to introduce self- and peer-assessment. Race (1998) also contains some suggestions for getting the most out of peer-assessment such as, allow time for the assessment exercise and the need to keep everyone well informed.

Follow-up and evaluation

Try not to give feedback on the process to the group or individual, but do discuss feedback with students — and receive it, from them. Exchange views with your students as to how the process went. Listen to what value it had for them. Remember, this is an inclusive process. Try not to leave them with a void. Attempt to identify any concerns or problems, which may mean alteration to how self- and peer-assessment may be used next time. Use a detailed and diverse form of evaluation methodology, such as questionnaires and group interviews.

A number of the case studies included in this book have thoughtful guidance on preparing and implementing self- and peer-assessment; Hughes's contribution (Case Study 5) is particularly helpful. The importance of careful consideration of preparation, implementation and evaluation cannot be over emphasised. The consequences of not doing this may lead to ineptly introduced and delivered practices that produce results directly opposite of what is desired.

SELF- AND PEER-ASSESSMENT: A COMMUNITY OF PRACTICE

Encouraging students to engage in self- and peer-assessment

A barrier to new methods of assessment are an individual's prior experience of being assessed. Hence it is necessary to consider how to encourage students to be involved. Be aware of the problems that students may have. Cheng and Warren, (1997) highlighted some student concerns. Students may:

- be aware of their own shortcomings in the subject area;

- have doubts about their own objectivity; and

- feel that the process is unfair.

Often tutors are regarded as specialists in their field, which could mean that students feel more inadequate as they are novices to the subject and therefore in awe of staff. This should be avoided as much as possible and the role of tutors should be more as guides. This is one reason why a different non-specialist tutor should facilitate in some of the implementation.

(Falchikov, 2003) highlighted other concerns such as.

- Social effects, such as friendships or hostility.

- It is the 'job' of the teacher to mark work.

It may, therefore, be necessary to 'sell' to the students the idea that their involvement in assessment is a good thing. There are a number of considerations to remember.

- Ensure students feel 'safe' about the process. Sullivan and Hall (1997) considered this an important issue.

- In peer-assessment, it may be necessary to make the process as anonymous as possible (Merry and Orsmond, Case Study 1).

- In order to engage students, teachers need to clearly identify why they want students to be involved in the assessment process. Students need to see the value (what's in it for them) of engaging in a particular form of self- or peer-assessment. The case study by Hughes (Case Study 5) has some useful suggestions as to why students need to be involved.

- Show students (and other staff) the research literature as the evidence that it works. Also it may help to introduce students to theories of learning, perhaps discuss with them the Zone of Proximal Development (see Chapter 1) and illustrate how self- and peer-assessment are interventions to enhance their learning.

- Use exemplars as a practice run for the students, so that they can gain objective confidence. Exemplars allow students to understand and use the concepts and criteria with the guidance of their tutor and additional input of peers at the beginning of a project or course. These exemplars may normally be work gen-erated from previous cohorts of students who undertook a similar assessment. A number of case studies in this guide advocate the use of exemplars, Brennan et al. (Case Study 7) is one such example.

Encouraging teachers to engage in offering and using self- and peer-assessment

It is important to encourage colleagues to be involved in alternative forms of assessment. There are a number of reasons for this.

- Within modular and distance-learning frame-works assessment communities are becoming increasingly fragmented.

- Increasingly, assessment involves more than just one person, or even one subject area.

- This greater involvement will challenge tacit notions of standards shared in a familiar academic community (Ecclestone, 2001).

- The one-off experience is not good. There is a need for practice if skills in assessing their own work or that of peers are to be developed and integrated into students' normal learning patterns.

- Students should have peer-assessment and exemplar work available to support their ongoing self- and peer-assessment practice, enabling and empowering them to achieve higher standards of learning, and therefore higher success in their studies.

Falchikov (2003) gave some suggestions as to how colleagues' suspicions and hostility can be overcome.

- Help allay fears of colleagues by informing them about existing research that advises on best practice.

- Consider using assessment for formative purposes.

- Help ease the change of role required, by stressing the importance of the teacher in setting up, implementing and running a self- or peer-assessment initiative, and in helping students acquire the necessary expertise.

SUMMARY

Achieving empowerment for students in assessment processes demands their involvement with the assessment marking criteria. Although desirable, it is not always possible to have students involved in criteria construction. However, the onus is on the tutor to ensure that students have a good working understanding of the criteria. The design of the marking criteria often involves discussion of learning outcomes. Therefore it is one of the cornerstones to preparing students for assessment and a valuable tool in successful implementation of self- and peer-assessment. How we 'get started' and 'keep going' with self- and peer-assessment involves a lot of effort, reflection and planning on behalf of tutors. This is well illustrated in the Cogdell *et al.,* case study (Case Study 4). To have a truly effective impact on student learning requires departments and faculties to take on board both the culture and underlying philosophies of self- and peer-assessment; students need to perceive this form of assessment as a natural process in their learning and be actively involved in its implementation and its importance in lifelong learning.

3

GOING DEEPER

SELF- AND PEER-ASSESSMENT: A ROLE IN A SUPERCOMPLEX WORLD

Introducing supercomplexity

Chapter 1 introduced the learning society, one where skilled and flexible learners are required. Learning was seen as a continual process throughout life. Barnett (2000) begins to give some shape to the type of world higher education may have to prepare students for. He described the world we live in as complex one, where we are assailed by more facts, data, evidence and arguments than we can easily handle. However, the world that current students may one day be entering is not a complex world, but rather a supercomplex world. One where everyone is continually being conceptually challenged, and through these challenges able to discover the way that they understand themselves, the world, and how secure they feel about acting in the world. Supercomplexity is already recognisable in the world of work through terms such as 'flexibility', 'adaptability' and 'self-reliance'. The implication of this terminology is that individuals have to take responsibility for 'continually reconstituting' themselves. In other words, tutors will have to think more about the society we are becoming, their role in the work place, and how they can make any necessary changes. To prepare graduates to meet the challenge and to prosper in a supercomplex world requires a curriculum which fully embraces the domains of being, knowing and action.

Powerful learning environments

On first encountering the literature regarding complex worlds the reader is immediately aware of the role which self- and peer-assessment can play. This is well illustrated in a study by Schelfhout *et al.* (2004) who described a powerful learning environment which is aimed at fostering entrepreneurial skills and incorporated elements of self-, peer- and teacher-assessment. The design principles behind powerful learning environments such as supporting constructive learning processes, resonate as the core principles of self- and peer-assessment. One prime reason for using self- and peer-assessment relates to the use of feedback, 'Within the learning process it is important to give students feedback in a way that challenges their perception on how to behave within groups (learning to cooperate, organise etc.). A combination of self-, peer- and coach-assessments, followed by group discussions can be used'. Here we are reminded of Vygotsky's theories of learning discussed in Chapter 1. When tutors and students are involved in assessment, it is often referred to as co-assessment or collaborative assessment (Dochy *et al.,* 1999).

Problem-based learning (PBL) potentially allows for the creation of a powerful learning environment, developing abilities and assessing them, as it does cognitive, metacognitive (heightened awareness of one's own learning through developed cognitive processes) and social competencies. Self- and/or peer-assessment are good sources of assessment for PBL, as marking criteria often need to be developed and implemented in the judging of the learning process or product. However, PBL incorporating self- and peer-assessment is not without its difficulties, as reported by Segers and Dochy (2001). They found rather mixed results. Students involved in the study were new to both PBL and self- and peer-assessment. As a result there were a number of issues raised in the study that would be helpful to those considering similar approaches:

- there were concerns about the comments of peers;

- the criteria were felt difficult to interpret;

- the self- and peer-assessment process was not sufficiently introduced; and

- students tended not to be able to reflect on their own functioning.

The authors saw these problems in a positive fashion, identifying room for teachers to improve their educational practice and to look again at the alignment of assessment with the main goals of the programme, with specific attention to certain issues like critical reflection.

Jackson and Ward (2004) outlined a way of representing complex learning suitable for meeting the demands of a supercomplex world. They described how higher education curricula can reflect the disciplinary world of knowledge and the world of professional and work-based learning. They proposed five different curriculum-assessment environments, one of which, the 'explicit curriculum', allows students to recognise and record their own learning and achievement through Personal Development Planning (PDP). PDP may have a number of different focuses, such as encouraging students to take responsibility for their own learning, and encouraging students to understand more fully the process of learning as discussed earlier in this book. Self-assessment is seen as a universal assessment concept within these processes.

SELF- AND PEER-ASSESSMENT: ENGAGEMENT IN REFLECTION

While tutors can choose to become more effective reflective teachers as opposed to good teachers (Kuit et al., 2001) it is likely that many tutors will have to facilitate reflective practice in students as part of students' Personal Development Planning. Reflection is a very important part of development planning. As considered by Moon (2001) reflection is 'a means of working on what we know already, thoughts, ideas, feelings, we may add new information and then we draw out of it something that accords with the purpose for which we reflected'. Adding new information may take place as a solitary process, or it may involve other people. The latter can lead to the development of a learning conversation where discussion may focus on learning experiences in which the learner reflects on some event or activity (Candy et al., 1985).

The learning experiences, which might feed reflections, are given consideration by Schön (1983). Schön moved the reader from thinking about the concept of knowing-in-action to reflecting-in-action. Knowing-in-action relates to how people in daily life intuitively perform the actions of everyday life. When someone reflects on the situations in which they are performing, and on the know-how implicit in their performances, they are, in some cases, reflecting-in-action. Schön accepted that reflecting-in-action may not always be possible, but that these arguments admit the possibility of reflecting-on-action, that is, looking back on an experience where reflecting-in-action was not possible. Pereira (1999) and Cowan (2002) give good examples of both reflection-in-action and reflection-on-action.

Cowan (2002) identifies a third type of reflection which he called reflection-for-action. Cowan explained that this type of reflection may occur at the start of a reflective process, where aspirations are being defined or problems are being identified with the hope of finding a resolution. This type of reflection is anticipatory and establishes priorities to support subsequent learning.

Proposing a model for carrying out reflective practice, Cowan (2002) brought together the interpretation of reflection as given by Schön (whichever variant), which Cowan considered to be open-ended activity, with reflection (as interpreted by Kolb in his learning cycle), which Cowan considered to be closed, as it is part of a sequence and as such, may act as a bridge to cross between sequences. Cowan's model, therefore, is one which incorporates reflection- for-, in-, and on-action.

Further refinement of reflective practice has allowed Cowan to develop models for 'analytical' and 'evaluative' reflection.

In analytical reflection, Cowan (2002) took analysis to be a cognitive process in which it is useful to look for patterns and generalities. These then, help learning concerning a particular experience. In evaluative reflection, Cowan addressed questions such as 'How well can I do it?' or 'Should I do it better?'

Self-assessment and peer review within a reflective framework, is well illustrated by Cowan (2002). The example involved the generation of learning contracts, which required students on a weekly basis to summarise their individual personal learning objectives for that week and to produce an outline of the methods they proposed to use in order to achieve those objectives. Each student had to ask another student to comment on their personal objectives. Students were then required to consider these comments carefully but did not necessarily have to agree with them. At the end of each week, each student was asked to produce something which demonstrated what he or she had learnt. At the end of term, students self-assessed their work by:

- summarising the standards and criteria, which they had been striving to achieve;

- describing their performance in comparable terms; and

- reporting on the process of judgement by which they compared their performance with their criteria and standards.

Asking students to make their assessment judgement in this way illustrates an important component of self-assessment, providing the equal emphasis on process awareness and development as well as on the rigorous content coverage. Their final mark was awarded against the outcome of their summative judgement, providing that all agreements in the learning contract had been met. In this way, Cowan saw this example of self-assessment involving:

- the year long experience being predominantly reflection-in-action;

- the end of term's assessments being reflection-on-action; and

- the end of term assessments, as they were completed, being reflection-for-action.

FORMATIVE ASSESSMENT AND SUMMATIVE ASSESSMENT: A ROLE FOR SELF- AND PEER-ASSESSMENT

Formative assessment

Sadler (1989) introduced the reader to formative assessment by considering the adjective formative. This implies the forming or moulding of something, usually to achieve a desired end. This is important to bear in mind, as often what is called formative assessment is nothing more than an arrangement of a set of multiple summative assessment tasks, described as if their main function was feedback, but with a considerable direct influence on the final outcome mark (Cowan 2002). Formative assessment contributes to learning by short-circuiting the randomness and inefficiency of trial and error learning. It is concerned with how judgements about the quality of student responses are shaping learning (Sadler, 1989).

Formative assessment is carried out in a series of specific stages. Students undertake an assessed assignment. They then receive formative feedback, feedback designed to inform them about their performance, and the judgement of it. Learning takes place and student performance is assessed again. Thus feedback is the key element in formative assessment, and feedback is often defined in terms of 'information about the gap between the actual level and the reference level of a system parameter which is used to alter the gap in some way' (Ramaprasad, 1983). Sadler stressed the active closing of the gap, rather than feedback being by nature for information. For learning to take place, the gap between the student performance before and after feedback and the performance after feedback must close. Sadler (1989) argued that there are three conditions for effective feedback. Students must be able to:

- monitor their own work;

- appreciate work of high quality; and

- judge (objectively) their product in comparison.

Furthermore, in keeping with good self- and peer-assessment practice, Sadler stressed the importance of ownership of a goal (the degree of performance or excellence achieved) as playing a significant part in the voluntary regulation of performance and the involvement of students in using multi-criterion judgements.

A study illustrating the implementation of a formative assessment exercise of histology posters is described by Orsmond et al., (2004). There were a number of stages involved in this study, the key components of which were.

- Students constructed criteria for marking a histology poster which had been made by a student from a previous cohort. This was the exemplar poster.

- Students were then given two criteria by the tutors. Unknown to the students, the tutors had constructed one 'worthwhile' criterion and one 'ambiguous' criterion. Students working in pairs or trios were given copies of both criteria by tutors and were asked to mark an exemplar poster.

- Tutors then marked the poster using both criteria.

- Tutors then discussed with students groups: (1) the criteria that the students had constructed earlier in the session, (2) the 'worthwhile' criterion and 'ambiguous' one, (3) the marking process, (4) further developments regarding the concept of marking criteria.

- Tutors listened to the student's perceptions of marking criteria and attempted to clarify any misconceptions.

- Tutors then discussed among themselves their individual discussions with student groups.

- Students and tutors wrote down agreed criteria along with definitions.

- A week later the tutors and students met again in the same pairs or trios. Students constructed posters and marked the posters using the criteria that had been jointly constructed with the tutor.

- Students self-assessed their own poster and peer-assessed those of their colleagues.

In this study students were able to engage in formative learning activities which required (1) discussions with their peers and tutors, (2) self-reflection, (3) self- and peer-assessment. Overall the students found the process very beneficial with the majority of the students responding in a positive way.

Complex learning can be more readily accomplished working with others, where, for example, alternative interpretation of tasks or situations is required (Boud, 2000). Working with others strongly encourages a more formative learning environment, incorporating both formative assessment and formative feedback. Support by peers is seen as very important because of the autonomy expected in higher education. There is good evidence that students help each other, but are not seen as replacements for staff (Drew, 2001).

For some, a problem for higher education is that traditional forms of summative assessment are being stretched to cover learning outcomes that resist robust, reliable and affordable summation (Knight, 2002). Rather than live with the difficulties, Knight and Yorke (2003) argued that greater use be made of formative assessment. Complex learning outcomes are also encountered where, through genuine discussion, sub-groups of outcomes can be generated as in claim-making. In making a claim, students 'claim' against the expectations set for the programme of study and justify these claims with evidence. Claim making encourages reflective practice, evaluation of learning and links in well with PDP (Knight and Yorke, 2003).

Summative assessment: the use of self- and peer-assessment

Not everyone perceives the problems of summative assessment to be as extensive as Knight and Yorke. A more pressing concern is that because of its extensive use, summative assessment may, in some way, suppress the use of formative assessment. Thus it is important to maintain a balance between the two forms of assessment (Boud and Falchikov, 2004) and where possible integrate self- and peer-assessment. Taras (2001) advocated an interesting form of self-assessment with a summative end-point. Students submit a summative piece of work, this is marked and given written feedback by the tutor. The work is returned, but the mark withheld. The students work through the tutor feedback, through group/class discussions, and then self- and possibly peer-assessment. Students are then asked to:

- Judge their work against an agreed criteria.

- Explain how they would improve a comparable piece of work in future.

- Grade their work.

Tutors collect the students' comments and grades. The tutors then feedback how well they think the students have addressed the criteria, and provide the tutor grade. The process of self-assessment is dependent on tutor and possible peer feedback. The value of self-assessment with and without feedback provides an interesting insight into the process of assessment and has been further developed by Taras (2003).

A detailed study looking at summative assessment in biosciences is reported by Butcher *et al.*, (1995). Here both the process and product of group projects were assessed. Overall six separate assessments of performance were made. The work is interesting for a variety of reasons. It discussed issues surrounding the arrival of a single student assessment grade, with particular reference to assessment weightings. It is also a good example of authentic assessment practice, in that students undertook an assessment task that resembled assignments undertaken by professional biologists, in this case, solving an industrial problem within certain resource constraints. The case study by Brennan *et al.*, (Case Study 7) also has an emphasis on such authentic assessment.

A way of balancing formative and summative assessment is discussed by Nieweg (2004). This paper, relating to learning in physiotherapy, illustrates how self-assessment can be used in conjunction with summative assessments. It also provides an opportunity to consider using formatively assessed assignments in an authentic, realistic and meaningful way by involving external clients to give feedback.

SELF-EVALUATION OR SELF-ASSESSMENT: CONSIDERING A RICH DIVERSITY OF APPROACHES

So far in this book we have considered self-assessment within fairly well defined parameters, perhaps too well defined. Klenowski (1995), considered self-evaluation, in terms of 'the evaluation or judgement of the worth of one's performance and the identification of one's strengths and weakness with the view to improving one's learning outcomes.' Therefore, as Klenowski, explained, 'self-evaluation is used in a broader sense than student self-assessment because it refers to ascribing value to the learning experience: first, by the identification of the criteria used; second, by indicating what is considered meritorious; and third, by outlining the implications for future action.' In other words, students see what is good in their work and should come to know how to make it better. Students use the outcomes of discussions or perhaps reflections in their development and achieve higher learning outcomes. Self-evaluation is being used in 'a formative context in meeting a self-development learning function. It is a

self-evaluation to open up some interesting questions about the nature and function of self-assessment. Claxton had broad sympathy with Klenowski, but had two caveats. Firstly he stated 'mere clarification of external criteria of assessment does not develop learning acumen, though it may raise attainment'. Claxton seemed to be covering all options with the inclusion of the word 'mere'. However, the point that raising attainment is not necessarily linked to developing learning acumen is important. The other caveat, that discussion of criteria needs to be considered on 'the road towards developing an ability that is essentially intuitive', is very important. Intuitive learning is an often complex and may imply finely tailored understanding.

A comparison of the work of Klenowski, Claxton, Boud, Cowan and Sadler can be very helpful in allowing us to appreciate the rich diversity of thinking and approaches taken towards students learning, which may have implication for those implementing self- and peer-assessment. Just considering one aspect of the formative assessment process, can show rich diversity of thought, see Table 2 below.

TABLE 2. A COMPARISON OF ATTITUDES BY KLENOWSKI, CLAXTON AND SADLER IN ONE ASPECT OF COMMUNICATING WITH STUDENTS IN A FORMATIVE SETTING

Klenowski	Claxton	Sadler
Perceptive, guided thought about each other's work may increase 'self-awareness' or progress in learning. Self-evaluation in relation to identified criteria is best.	Self-assessment using externally specified criteria, can be irrelevant, even counter productive to learning acumen. Self-evaluation is intuitive and hindered by checklist criteria.	Strictly speaking, all methods of grading that emphasise ranking or comparison among students are irrelevant for formative purposes.

process of identifying the value of the teaching and learning experience for the individual student'.

For some, it may therefore be difficult to see how self-assessment and self-evaluation differ. Cowan (2002) employed the term 'evaluation' to describe a 'process' in which judgements are made by comparing performances with criteria or standards. Cowan restricted the term 'assessment' to evaluation which concentrates on an outcome, in the form of a grade or mark or judgement, whether formative or summative'. Klenowski, used the term 'evaluation', and generated a formal grade that was recorded.

This is more than idle banter over words. Searching for meaningful distinctions between terms can provide the opportunity for enquiry into some key aspects of the assessment process. Claxton (1995), commenting on the Klenowski paper, considered

SELF- AND PEER-ASSESSMENT: STUDENTS AND TUTORS PERCEPTION

Students' perceptions
Student perceptions of self-assessment are illustrated well by Cowan et al., (1999) who studied how self-assessment can be used in the summative assessment of reflective journals and self-assessment. The paper is richly embroidered with quotes from students, which readily allow the reader to share their experiences over a year of self-assessment. For example, in this quote you really feel the exacting demands being made. 'I knew instantly that self-assessment was going to be a problem for me. I just did not know how I was going to devise a criterion to begin with, let alone assess myself'. However, while students continued to find the self-assessment

challenging they were able to comment at the end 'self-assessment did make me realise that I need to develop myself further into being more critical of my work. I tend to rely too much on feedback rather than critically evaluating myself. Self-assessment did give me the opportunity to question this'. The influence of peers was also noted in a positive way 'having to justify why I thought some aspects of the journal was really good was perhaps more difficult than saying why it was bad. It was useful having a colleague commenting on this — even if it was rather unnerving. It has been a very trusting relationship and the need for confidentiality is essential'. Sometimes the perceptions are not always viewed in a positive light, even if the process does provide a better measure of learning, such as this quote on alternative assessment methods; 'I think it tests you better, because it's not just testing your memory, it's testing your knowledge of the subject. It's all about ... being able to interpret and put your own point of view. It's a bit unfortunate, really, isn't it' Sambell *et al.,* (1997). In this Guide, comments on student's perceptions of peer-assessment are included in the case study by Rushton *et al.*, (Case Study 3).

Tutors' perceptions

Maclellan (2001) carried out a study into assessment for learning to evaluate the different perceptions of student and tutors. The tutors perceived the primary purpose of assessment was to grade or rank students, but the more developmental purposes were not discounted. However, the importance placed on the developmental formative role is not internally consistent with other views endorsed by staff. For example.

- Assessment neither took place at the start, nor could students be assessed when they felt ready.

- Self- and peer-assessment were infrequent.

Nevertheless, declarative knowledge *per se* was not the sole purpose and functional knowledge such as, formulating ideas was assessed. However, the extent to which assessment genuinely focused on students' capacity to apply, transform or evaluate the relevance of declarative knowledge in different situations could be viewed as question-able, when considering the processes through which assessment information was gathered.

SUMMARY

Very few people have a neutral view on assessment. This is because it is such an emotive issue; as indicated by many of the student quotes throughout the book.

In self- and peer-assessment, students may need to explore, at different times, rather complex emotions about themselves and what it is that they may become. The issues, which increasingly tutors are asking students to engage with are huge; and lots of students struggle to 'get their heads round them'. Self- and peer-assessment provide students, as well as tutors the opportunity to 'touch base'. At the start of their learning journey students ask their tutors questions like 'is this what you mean?' By the end of the journey, students are asking questions of themselves and seeking self justification for what they have learned.

CLOSING THOUGHTS

The old adage 'you can take a horse to water but you can't make it drink' seems lost on many in higher education who spend their time 'teaching' students rather than allowing them to 'learn'. As a result, a lot of time and money is spent assessing superficial learning. Early in Chapter 1, reference was made to Rogers' perception of the goals of education (Rogers, 2003). These goals were strongly student-centred, and as Rogers admitted 'even in our own culture these are functional goals of very few educators'. For Rogers, writing in the early 1950's, education appeared to be operationally based on the assumption 'you can't trust the student... the teacher needs to supply everything'. However, Rogers steadfastly believed you could trust the student to learn in a way which will maintain or enhance self. Boud and Falchikov (2004) considered assessment and write of their dismay at 'practice inconsistent with research in higher education and indeed institutional policy'.

Sadly, for many, very little seems to have changed in the intervening years, and we need to begin to question why this is. For those who have always had a strong interest in student-centred learning, the trend of the self remaining central to learning and assessment persists. This book documents case studies and educational research by people with a genuine concern for meaningful assessment, both of and for learning. We continue to seek some reform of many established, but outdated practices, as Rogers did; and we need to be strong advocates for student-centred assessment, which goes beyond the superficial.

BIOSCIENCE CASE STUDIES

The following section contains a collection of seven bioscience case studies. All the case studies have been written by bioscientists who have implemented self- and/or peer-assessment into their own teaching. The case studies are organised around common headings ('Background and rationale', 'Advice', 'Troubleshooting', 'Does it work?' and 'Further Developments'), but each study reflects the author's individual style and preference.

CASE STUDY 1
THE EFFECT OF MARKING CRITERIA AND EXEMPLARS ON STUDENTS' LEARNING
DURING PEER- AND SELF-ASSESSMENT OF SCIENTIFIC POSTERS
Stephen Merry & Paul Orsmond Faculty of Health and Sciences, Staffordshire University,
Stoke-on-Trent ST4 2DE. *Email: s.merry@staffs.ac.uk*

CASE STUDY 2
ON-LINE CALIBRATED PEER-ASSESSMENT — STUDENT LEARNING BY MARKING ASSIGNMENTS
Victor Kuri School of Biological Sciences at Seale Hayne (Food Technology), Seale-Hayne Campus,
University of Plymouth, Newton Abbot TQ12 6NQ. *Email: V.Kuri@plymouth.ac.uk*

CASE STUDY 3
PEER-ASSESSMENT OF SCIENTIFIC POSTERS — THE LEAGUE FIXTURE APPROACH
Brian Rushton School of Environmental Science, University of Ulster,
Coleraine, Northern Ireland, BT52 1SA. *Email: BS.Rushton@ulster.ac.uk*

CASE STUDY 4
PEER-ASSESSMENT OF GROUP WORK IN A LARGE CLASS —
DEVELOPMENT OF A STAFF AND STUDENT FRIENDLY SYSTEM
Barbara Cogdell, Andrea Brown & Ailsa Campbell Institute of Biomedical and Life Sciences,
University of Glasgow, Glasgow G12 8QQ. *Email: B.Cogdell@bio.gla.ac.uk*

CASE STUDY 5
PEER-ASSESSMENT OF PRACTICAL WRITE-UPS USING AN EXPLICIT MARKING SCHEDULE
Ian Hughes School of Biomedical Sciences, University of Leeds, Leeds LS2 9JT.
Email: i.e.hughes@leeds.ac.uk

CASE STUDY 6
WRITING AND REVIEWING AN ARTICLE FOR A SCIENTIFIC MAGAZINE —
A PEER/SELF-ASSESSMENT EXERCISE
Rob Reed Division of Biomedical Sciences, Northumbria University,
Newcastle-upon-Tyne NE1 8ST. *Email: rob.reed@unn.ac.uk*

CASE STUDY 7
PEER-ASSESSED PROBLEM-BASED CASE STUDIES
Charles Brennan, Elizabeth Folland, Rick Preston & Nicola Blatchford
School of Biological Sciences at Seale Hayne (Food Technology), Seale-Hayne Campus,
University of Plymouth, Newton Abbot TQ12 6NQ. *Email: c.s.brennan@massey.ac.nz*

It is hoped that these cases studies will provide guidance, inspiration, as well as practical advice on how to implement self- and/or peer-assessment in the biosciences. There is also a accompanying website to this guide (http://www.bioscience.heacademy.ac.uk/TeachingGuides/). The website contains a further practical material to aid the reader in implementing self- and/or peer-assessment. The site includes expanded versions of the case studies, further bioscience case studies, explicit marking schedules and criteria to download, as well as video streams of peer-assessment.

1

The effect of marking criteria and exemplars on students' learning during peer- and self-assessment of scientific posters

STEPHEN MERRY & PAUL ORSMOND

 BACKGROUND AND RATIONALE

The authors of this report are practicing lecturers with an interest in the influence that assessment practices have on the way that students learn. This "case study" is the combination of four studies investigating student and tutor perceptions of poster marking criteria at Level 1 undergraduate modules within the general field of Biology. Self- and peer-assessment exercises of the students' completed posters together with organised, but informal, formative feedback sessions were used to provide data concerning students' and tutors' perceptions of marking criteria.

The precise learning outcomes of the component individual studies differed, but overall it can be stated that, *'at the end of their participation students should be able to'*:

- explain the meaning of specific marking criteria in a professional biological context;

- provide appropriate formative feedback to colleagues concerning their performance;

- engage meaningfully in the process of peer review as used by professional biologists;

- reflect more on the assessment process as part of their own learning and thereby enhance their learning.

 'HOW TO DO IT'

The formats of the four studies were similar, but not

identical. The approach described below is a composite which reflects how we would now run such a study.

Stage 1
(4–6 weeks before the poster assessment exercise)
Students were informed that:

- they were required to make a scientific poster, the date of the poster assessment exercise and the topic of the poster;

- posters are a recognised format in which scientific researchers present their results i.e. the assessment was relevant;

- they were required to supply particular materials (i.e. paper headings, adhesives etc) in order to construct their poster and the size of the poster boards;

- they would work in groups of approximately five to discuss the marking criteria, but they would be required to produce individual posters;

- more details would be provided at a later date.

Stage 2
(3–4 weeks before the poster assessment exercise)
Either students were informed what the marking criteria were (if they were tutor provided) and were then allowed time (approximately 30 minutes) to discuss the meaning of the marking criteria in their groups with tutors circulating among the groups to contribute to the discussions.

Or students were allowed time (approximately 45 minutes) to work in their groups to both generate, discuss and refine their own poster marking criteria and agree them with tutors circulating among the groups during this process.

Students were then informed that:

- they would be required to peer-assess the posters of others and self-assess their own posters using the marking criteria they had just discussed and that tutors would also assess the posters using the same marking criteria;

- anonymous peer review was a process utilised by professional scientists which was fundamental to establishing the credibility of scientific publications i.e. they were engaging in genuine professional practice;

- they should regard the self- and peer-assessment activity as a vehicle for developing specific skills such as self reflection and objective judgement required by professional biologists;

- their posters were to be presented anonymously to reduce any bias in the assessment;

- their self- and peer-assessment would contribute to the overall grades awarded for the exercise and that tutors were interested in the quality of comments made by students in addition to their accuracy of their marking compared to that of tutors;

- more information would be provided at a later date.

Stage 3
(1–2 weeks before the poster assessment exercise)

- Students were given written information concerning the meaning of the individual marking criteria. This information was influenced by the discussions that had previously taken place between tutors and students. It should point out both the meaning of the criteria and the misconceptions which some students seemed to have.

- Students were also given a copy of the marking form they would be required to use for the self- and peer-assessment of their posters and its use was discussed with them, paying particular attention to they types and usefulness of the feedback comments they might provide to their peers.

- Students were given the opportunity to view exemplar posters and to discuss them in their groups and with circulating tutors. They should decide what feedback they would give to the author of the poster and what grades they would award for each marking criterion.

- If student-derived criteria are being used to mark the posters, students should be given, in discussion with tutors, the opportunity to refine the criteria; although such changes should be agreed and discussed with the whole class since changes to the written information provided may be required.

- Students were reminded of the date and time of the poster construction and assessment exercise together with the materials they would need to bring to the session in order to construct their poster, and the time they have available (i.e. 30 minutes) for poster construction.

Stage 4
(The poster assessment exercise)
In an initial plenary session students were informed:

- they will be randomly allocated to two rooms;

- they will be given coloured stickers to attach to their posters;

- they will be given 30 minutes to construct their posters before the start of the self- and peer-assessment exercise;

- they will be required to self-assess their own posters and then move to the other room where they are required to peer-assess all the posters having the same coloured sticker as their own;

- their self- and peer-assessment marking should be independent, i.e. they should not discuss their marks and comments with other students; although tutors were available to provide guidance regarding the usage of the marking forms;

- tutors were interested in the quality of feedback comments as much as the grades awarded;

- in their poster construction they should ensure that only their student number appears on the poster NOT their name.

At the end of the plenary session students were allocated to their rooms and given their individual coloured stickers to attach to their completed posters.

- The format was as described in the introductory plenary;

- Packs of marking forms (one form for each poster to be assessed) were made available to students at the commencement of the self- and peer-assessment exercise;

- At the end of the session tutors collected in the completed marking forms and elicited any informal feedback on their experience of the assessment process from individual students to enable the procedures to be refined for subsequent cohorts.

ADVICE ON USING THIS APPROACH

Tutor discussion with students is the key to the success of the exercise. Tutor discussion should provide to students a) feedback regarding their interpretation and use of marking criteria and b) reassurance that they do have the ability to judge the scientific quality of a poster without the background knowledge necessary to judge the accuracy of the factual detail provided within it.

Posters produced by previous cohorts of students are a good source or exemplars. Students should be given the opportunity to view posters of differing styles and quality. It can help some students realise that attractive posters may, in some cases, have poor scientific depth.

If a sequential allocation of students to rooms and to peer-assessment groups (i.e. a sequential allocation of different coloured stickers) is adopted and these are allocated to students in turn as they leave the plenary session this helps ensure that friendship groups (who are likely to leave together) are separated during the assessment process.

In a 1-hour self- and peer-assessment exercise students should be asked to grade and provide feedback on a maximum of five posters; including their own. This is to enable them sufficient time to write meaningful feedback comments. The number of peer-assessment groups, i.e. the number of different coloured stickers used, should reflect this.

Self- and peer-assessment are skills that improve with practice. Furthermore, informal feedback from students has indicated that they are more willing to engage with the process at a deeper level if they meet it on a second occasion. If possible, repeated self- and peer-assessment exercises should be built into the curriculum rather than being delivered as single isolated events.

 ### TROUBLESHOOTING

In some instances students were unwilling to award low grades, even if they thought they were deserved, to posters that they recognised as being those of their close colleagues. Furthermore, in discussions approximately one month after the completion of the exercise individual students have informed tutors that they felt other students (to whom they did award a low grade) were behaving differently towards them. To address this, tutors need to ensure posters are as anonymous as possible and that friendship groups are distributed into different peer-assessment groups.

Students do find the process challenging. This can be a surprise if they have initially a superficial view of presenting information in poster format.

Furthermore, some students feel they are not able to judge the scientific merit of posters whose topic is not strictly the same as theirs. They need reassurance and guidance that they can judge the scientific merit of a poster without being able to judge the accuracy of the detail present in the content.

Finally some students can treat the process in a rather cavalier fashion. Emphasising at the start that they are engaging in a practice which is employed by professional biologists to establish the credibility of their work helps to dispel this.

 ### DOES IT WORK?

Both formal questionnaires and informal feedback from students have indicated that self- and peer-assessment exercises caused students to reflect more on the marking criteria and their learning (Orsmond et al., 1996; Orsmond et al., 1997; Orsmond et al., 2000; Orsmond et al., 2002; Orsmond et al., 2004). To this extent the approach does "work".

The ability of students to mark in an identical fashion to tutors should not be the sole criteria of success of self- and peer-assessment , but it can provide information as to the nature of the learning that is taking place. Our initial studies (Orsmond et al., 1996; Orsmond et al., 1997) demonstrated an overall agreement between student and tutor grades ($r^2 = 0.7$) comparable to that of other studies (Hughes and Large, 1993 and Stefani, 1992) with the agreement being greater for peer-assessment than for self-assessment. Consideration of the overall mark does, however, mask variations between tutor and student with regard to individual marking criteria. For example, students over-marked, compared to tutors for the criteria "visually effective" and "helpful level of detail", but under-marked for the criterion "clear and justified conclusion". The implication is that some students had written a clear and justified conclusion, but did not realise that they had done so. The necessity for dialogue with students concerning individual criteria was shown by these findings.

An interesting, and unexpected, outcome was that our studies, based on comparison of tutor and student grades, have indicated that the nature of the learning that has taken place differs dependent on whether the marking criteria are tutor-provided or student-derived (Orsmond et al., 2000). The use of student-derived criteria might be expected to circumvent discrepancies between tutors' and students' marks for individual criteria since tutors, with their greater experience of interpreting marking criteria, would be expected to more readily understand student-derived marking criteria than, possibly, students understand marking criteria provided by tutors. In our hands the outcome of using student-derived marking criteria was that students, although having ownership of marking criteria they had constructed themselves, were less able to discriminate between their own individual marking criteria than between those provided by tutors. Student groups either over-marked or under-marked all their marking criteria compared to tutors such that overall agreement between students' and tutors' marks was not enhanced. It may be that the act of constructing their own marking criteria caused students to view their posters in a more holistic fashion. An alternative interpretation of the finding is that students were able to interpret their marking criteria, but had a poor conception of the subject standards, i.e. both students and tutors knew what, for example, the marking criterion "self-explanatory" meant, but, despite the dialogue, they retained different conceptions of how self-explanatory the poster should be to achieve a particular grade.

Our final published study (Orsmond *et al.*, 2002) indicated that the use of exemplars was able to largely overcome discrepancies between grades awarded by students and tutors for student-derived marking criteria. The exemplars were posters produced by a previous cohort of students and served as a focus for discussion and application of the marking criteria. In addition to improving accuracy of marking for individual criteria, feedback from students indicated that the use of exemplars can help students' learning such that higher quality learning outcomes, including reflection, are achieved; although exemplars may not necessarily help students in the process of poster construction. A recent study (Orsmond *et al.*, 2004) has revealed that peer-assessing students were less able than tutors to write constructive feedback comments to the poster authors. Students' feedback comments concerned primarily the quality of the presentation of material with little actual mention as to whether the discussed marking criteria had been met. Tutors' comments, alternatively, concerned primarily the nature and use of the scientific content of the poster in the context of the marking criteria. A possible explanation for this is that students may focus, when constructing a poster, on the poster itself (i.e. the product of their work) whereas tutors may regard the poster simply as a means to enable students to demonstrate the understanding of science they have developed (i.e. to show the process that they have undergone).

In summary, the strengths of the approach are that it causes students to reflect more on their work and their learning, but for this to happen, careful planning is required together with the allocation of class time for the activities.

 FURTHER DEVELOPMENTS

The authors are currently investigating: How students' perceptions of marking criteria change during the course of the six week poster design and construction exercise; the type of distractions (i.e. student self-derived individual criteria that are distinct from the agreed marking criteria) which influence students' poster design and construction as well as how students use the feedback provided by tutors to enhance their learning.

2

Online calibrated peer-assessment — student learning by marking assignments

VICTOR KURI

 BACKGROUND AND RATIONALE

One of the first things that markers have to do to evaluate work is to agree a set of standards. Somehow lecturers have to develop an understanding of what is a good assignment, what is average and what is poor. When I collect a pile of assignments for marking in an area that I have not set before, the first thing that I do is to try to find some of the extremes, and 'calibrate' my marking scheme.

The use of 'calibrated' exemplars can help students become competent at peer review and understand what makes a good (and bad) assignment. I use the web-based Calibrated Peer Review (CPR) system which was developed on a science-based model of peer review (http://cpr.molsci.ucla.edu/). The system is anonymous and could be used on-line or with printouts during a timed session.

 'HOW TO DO IT'

Prepare an assignment brief, which ideally contains guidelines to set the criteria to which the work is going to be marked. It is best suited for text-based assignments, short and well structured.

Following preparation and submission of the text the student proceeds through calibration, peer-assessment, self-assessment and feedback, and results.

Calibration

Each student is presented with an assessment questionnaire and one script at the time. They have to use the questionnaire (assessment schedule) to evaluate and mark the script. At some points, they are encouraged to provide feedback. They do this for three scripts in a random order, which were prepared by the instructor and are standardised to be of low, medium and high quality. Feedback is provided to the students to verify how close they matched the calibration scripts. There is the facility for students to re-take the calibration to improve their marking proficiency.

Review

Each student is presented with a script from one of their peers, randomly selected and coded to keep it anonymous. They have to evaluate it and mark it following the questionnaire, where they also provide feedback. This is done for three students (the work of this assessor will be correspondingly marked by three randomly selected reviewers)

Self-assessment

Each student is given the opportunity to mark their own script following the same criteria. This mark will be part of the overall mark.

Feedback and results

The feedback information is made available to each student (keeping the markers anonymous) and a composite mark is computed to reflect the effort of the participants, considering that marking could be time consuming and challenging.

By the time the students finish they should have understood what was required in the assignment, marked seven scripts and have received feedback on their understanding of the assessment system, the requirements and their own compliance. This is a formative exercise which allows students the opportunity to understand and explore the peer-assessment process.

This system had been used with final year BSc and MSc students for a range of assignments, including a case study, short practical reports, discussion and conclusions of practicals, virtual poster displays and a reflective assignment exploring issues of food ethics. The briefing may involve instructions for the students to carry out an activity using a range of software, calculations, virtual (or laboratory) experiments, etc. Students have subsequently to write the outcome as a text report.

 ADVICE ON USING THIS APPROACH

Setting up the method can be time consuming, but once the assignments are designed, the system is easy to manage and the assignments can be administered to large groups with minimum effort. The on-line system does not work with files of web pages by itself, but it is possible to set up a repository of files or webpages (i.e student portal in the university intranet, or internet) and ask the students to input only the weblink to their work or a code to the file previously up-loaded by the instructor.

 TROUBLESHOOTING

The idea that the lecturer was not marking the assignment was alien to some of the students who felt uneasy because their peers were going to mark them. Others felt that they were not capable of marking assignments. A briefing session was introduced to manage students expectations and to motivate positive participation. Detailed instructions and a tutorial were set up to help students with limited IT skills.

One potential problem with the on-line CPR system is that the students obtain marks in ranges atypical for the group or university marking scheme. The marks can easily be normalised or the system re-set to provide different weighting for the text and each one of the tasks. Also, the threshold levels to give marks after successful completion of each task could be modified; i.e. if the self-assessment is less than 1.5 points from the reviewer's average mark (in a scale from 0–10), then 10 points are awarded, if it is >1.5 and >=2.5, 5 points but if it differs more that 2.5 points, then no points are awarded).

 DOES IT WORK?

The overall impact on students can be summarised as:

- Students realise that there are marking schemes and that these can help in achieving higher marks. Marking schemes also help them to focus their effort in further coursework.

- Students experience marking their peers and providing and receiving feedback to and from their peers.

- Some students enjoy being empowered to assess coursework and find it interesting and the responsibility challenging.

- The students learn by marking their peers work.

- Once students were reassured about the mechanics of the calibrated peer-assessment they understood the relevance of peer review.

- Some students welcomed the change, but most perceived the calibration and reviewing process just as extra work.

Aside from the improved student learning, one of the key benefits for staff is reduced workload in providing adequate and timely feedback to students.

3

Peer-assessment of scientific posters — the league fixture approach

BRIAN RUSHTON

BACKGROUND AND RATIONALE

Within the Biology degree at the University of Ulster, posters are used in many modules and training is provided in a Year One Transferable Skills module on the elements that go to make up a successful poster. One of the learning outcomes of the Transferable Skills module is to develop the students' critical abilities and peer-assessment of the posters was the vehicle used for this. Essentially, each student is asked to assess each poster independently using marking criteria that had been discussed with the class beforehand and the marks amalgamated and overall marks awarded that included an element from the tutor.

However, this did not prove entirely satisfactory. The workload for an individual student was high (typically between 10 and 18 posters) and also the students found it difficult marking to an absolute scale. The instructions required that the elements of the assessment be scored on a 0–10 scale with 4 being a pass mark. The concept of what constituted a fail was difficult and even the worst posters were given good pass marks.

It was important that the students saw, reviewed and criticised the work of their peers and therefore an alternative assessment strategy was introduced six years ago and has remained little changed. It is now used in two other modules as well, another Year One module, Biodiversity and a Year Two module, Biological Techniques and Analysis.

 'HOW TO DO IT'

The method currently used in the Transferable Skills module can be summarised as follows:

1. The Year One cohort usually consists of approximately 30 students but this number has been as high as 60+ in recent years. In week five of semester one, the students receive two sessions on the construction of posters — these focus on presentation and content. At the same time they are given the poster titles together with a few starter references. In previous years these have largely been related to popular issues in biology but this year, in anticipation of the introduction of Personal Development Planning, the emphasis was switched to careers and placements. Students form groups of three or four and work on their posters over the next few weeks and these are then displayed outside the main teaching laboratories during week eleven.

2. The poster in the Transferable Skills module is worth 10%. In other modules it may be higher (for example, in the Biodiversity module it is worth 15% with an associated seminar and log book of the process being worth a further 10%). A small number of marks are allocated for how conscientiously students have marked the posters.

3. Bearing in mind the difficulties outlined above when all students marked all posters, the process now involves:

   a. Each student is given a number of marking sheets. The number of sheets depends on the number of groups and the number of students but is usually two or three.

   b. Each marking sheet bears the titles (or numbers) of two of the posters on display but not including the poster of the group to which the student belongs.

   c. The rest of the marking sheet has a series of criteria divided into two categories, presentation and content; the student is expected to view the two posters and to make positive and negative comments under each heading for each of the two posters. The comments do not translate into a numeric score — this was where the students found real difficulty when they had to score the assessment criteria on a 0–10 basis.

d. Instead, after they have made their written comments, they have to state which poster is the best and to justify their decision on the basis of the individual comments they have made. This justification is no more than two to three sentences.

e. They are allowed to state that the two posters are equally good (or bad) if they really find it difficult to decide between them but they are strongly encouraged to 'find a winner'.

4. The marking sheets are designed like the games in a series of sports fixtures so that each poster 'plays' every other poster — the number of groups and the number of students will allow each poster to 'play' every other poster at least twice. For example if there are 40 students in groups of four there would be ten groups. For the whole 'fixture list' there would be 90 group comparisons (or 'games') with each student being responsible for two or three comparisons.

5. The 'winner' of a comparison is allocated two points, the loser none — with 'drawn' comparisons being allocated a point each (I haven't introduced the three points for a win and one point each for a draw system!) and the points totalled for each poster.

6. The posters are then ranked on the basis of the number of points awarded. At this stage it may be necessary to modify the points total if a student or students have failed to return the mark sheets — there are usually two or three students who opt out. Simply calculating the average number of 'points' awarded per 'game' is a simple solution to this problem.

7. I also mark the posters using my own assessment criteria and my marks and the students' points totals are amalgamated to give a final grade. I have experimented with a number of ways of doing this and the method currently used is to rank my marks and those of the students separately and add the two ranks together and allocate a grade and a percentage mark on the overall rank. Thus, the highest ranking poster would get an A and a mark of (say) 85%. Generally, posters do not fail!

 DOES IT WORK?

Overall, are students able to produce a sensible assessment of the posters? In Figure 1, the marks derived from the tutor (a percentage score) are plotted against the overall 'points' score of the class (adjusted for missing students) — the correlation coefficient is 0.800 (df = 13, p < 0.01) — suggesting that overall peer-assessment is remarkably consistent with the tutor's marks. Where there were significant discrepancies between tutor marks and those of the students this was usually for posters that had excellent presentation and poor content; in the students' minds the visual impact clearly outweighed the scientific content.

Correlation between tutor marks and those given by students are often low — several examples, drawn from a number of studies spanning a wide range of subject areas are discussed in Griffiths, Houston and Lazenbatt (1995). However, the usual approach adopted is for students to allocate marks on an absolute scale and this may explain the poor agreement compared with that reported here.

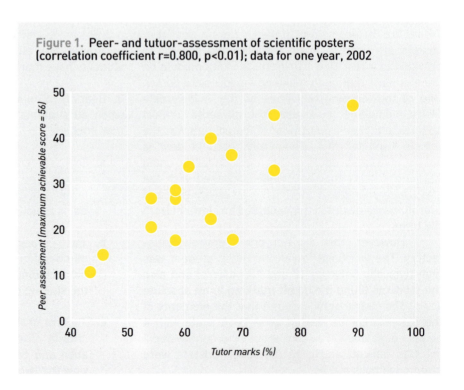

Figure 1. Peer- and tutuor-assessment of scientific posters (correlation coefficient r=0.800, p<0.01); data for one year, 2002

4

The students find this method of 'marking' much easier to cope with as they are simply making a judgement on which piece of work is best; they are not trying to use a numerical scale or mark against an absolute scale. This came out clearly in the module evaluation. It also means that they are focussing on a smaller number of posters and therefore more likely to learn and remember the content. One added advantage is that the mark sheets can be used directly as feedback to the groups.

WHAT DO THE STUDENTS THINK?

There is little doubt that peer-assessment is a valuable experience and is appreciated by students. In a previous peer tutoring and assessment exercise (Cook and Rushton, 1995) where Year Two students taught information technology skills (MS Word and Excel) to Year One students and then assessed them, the comments of the student tutors were very supportive of peer-assessment:

"Showed me how lazy and careless people could be with their work."

"Makes me reconsider and reassess my own work and the way I do it."

"It taught me ... how much better and assignment can look and read when more time is spent on it."

It would seem therefore to be a worthwhile exercise. However, it should not be seen as just an alternative to tutor marked assignments but should have clear, non-assessment outcomes — in this case, the development of critical faculties. As Biggs (1999) points out "Peer-assessment [is] not so much an assessment device, but a teaching-learning device."

ACCOMPANYING MATERIAL

The accompanying website to this guide (http://www.heabioscience.academy.ac.uk/TeachingGuides/) contains an extended version of this case study and the following additional material:

- notes on the assessment of posters;

- poster marking sheets.

Peer-assessment of group work in a large class — development of a staff and student friendly system

BARBARA COGDELL, ANDREA BROWN & AILSA CAMPBELL

 BACKGROUND AND RATIONALE

The first year biology course at the University of Glasgow is divided into two modules. Part of the assessment (20%) for the module in the second half of the year is a "Lifestyle Assignment". The subject specific aims are to investigate and evaluate the lifestyles of (a) species other than humans and (b) humans in other parts of the planet. A portion of the assessment is individual written work, but the majority of the marks are for the group work element of the Assignment.

There are two tasks for the group work, a debate and the manufacture of a poster. The debate is based on Darwin's dilemma. The students are required to argue the case for eliminating a species of their choice whose lifestyle is too damaging to the planet. Then they also argue the case for the preservation of another species chosen by another group. The second task is to produce a poster which compares the lifestyle of people in Britain with that of people in another country.

There are between 600 and 700 students taking the module. They are divided into 14 laboratory classes with roughly 48 students in each. Each of the lab classes is further divided into six groups of eight students — a total of 84 groups. The students have already worked together in the lab during the previous semester as they are always required to sit in the same lab position and they have already participated in a group discussion exercise. The groups meet both in scheduled lab sessions and in their own study time so that they can research their topics. Though the scheduled lab sessions are run by members of staff, the staff cannot monitor what happens when the students meet outside their lab sessions. The groups are encouraged to monitor themselves. Therefore they are required to elect a group leader and he/she is asked to make notes of who attended the sessions and who did what within the group.

The Lifestyle Assignment replaced a previous group work activity which was based on the theme of AIDS. There were continuous complaints that staff did not assess the group work that was required for the debates. Also group members did not like carrying non-contributors. During the last couple of years of the AIDS project, this resulted in a high proportion of the students failing to contribute to the debates.

It was decided in the Lifestyle Assignment to mark the group work to ensure motivation. It was also felt to be important to introduce a method of distinguishing individual contributions, i.e. to introduce peer-assessment. The method of peer-assessment has evolved over the three years of the Assignment's existence. Part of this has been enabled by the availability of appropriate technology.

Before the introduction of this peer-assessment to our Level 1 course our only experience of peer-assessment had been in a Level 2 Biology module. This had involved a much smaller number of students, 140 versus 650. Although the method of peer-assessment had been very successful it was considered unsuitable to be scaled up to a larger group. Therefore we looked for a system requiring less administrative time.

 ## YEAR 1 — KEEP THE ADMIN SIMPLE

Two members of staff gave each group a mark out of 100 for their debate and poster. The mark was multiplied by the number of members in the group. The group was told their total marks and they then had to divide the marks between themselves. So if the group had eight members and they were given a mark of 60, this gives a total mark for the group of 480. If they decided that they had all worked equally hard they could each get a final mark of 60% for the project. However if they decided two members of the group had worked particularly hard they could have more marks and if one person had done nothing they could agree to give that person 0. This might result in two members of the group getting 90%, five members getting 60% and one getting 0. A constraint was put that nobody could have over 100%.

The students allocated their marks together in a group in a scheduled lab session. Each group was given a single form with the full names and matriculation numbers of each of the members and a space to write their marks. At the end of the session the lab leader handed in the completed list of marks as communally agreed. Many groups agreed to share the marks equally amongst themselves.

This scheme was fairly simple to run as there was only one sheet of marks per group for staff to enter into the assessment spreadsheet. Checks were made to ensure that the students had made correct calculations. Any queries could be sorted by consultation with the group leader. Students awarded zero by their group were investigated by staff for extenuating circumstances such as illness.

However the students did not like this scheme at all. They did not like hammering out the marks in a group setting. They did not like giving low marks to colleagues face to face. Consequently non-contributors would get the same marks as everyone else and the rest of the group would feel resentful. Alternatively the group would mark a member down and this person would complain vociferously. In the worst cases groups split into two or three factions (this only happened on two or three occasions).

It is always to be expected that some groups will be dysfunctional. However with the large number of groups involved, and as the mark counts towards their final module mark, it is unrealistic to tell the groups that they should sort things out by themselves. The students have to be given marks, so this scheme resulted in a lot of extra work for the staff trying to monitor these problems.

 ## YEAR 2 — MAKE THE MARKING CONFIDENTIAL AND AUTOMATE THE MARKS CALCULATION

In the second year of the Lifestyle Assignment the department was fortunate to acquire an Intelligent Character Recognition (ICR) system. This machine will read forms with text entries. With the use of this technology it became feasible to get each student to submit a form with marks for each of the other members of their group. The forms are read automatically and marks entered into a spreadsheet. Then the subsequent calculations can be made automatically. Using individual forms meant we could change the peer-assessment protocol so that the students could give their marks for the other members of the group confidentially.

Each student was given a hard copy form with their name and matriculation number at the top. Below was a table with the names and matriculation numbers of the members of their group, not including themselves. The forms were generated using the mail merge function of Microsoft Word and Excel. Extra spaces were provided in case an extra student had joined the group without the teaching staff's knowledge. This could happen if a student was absent when the groups were formed or had completely failed to get on in an original group.

As before the debate and poster together were

given a mark out 100. Again this mark was multiplied by the number of students to give the total group marks. The students were asked to enter a mark out of 10 on their forms for each of their colleagues in the group. The forms were read by the machine and an average peer mark (out of 10) was calculated for each student. All the average marks for the whole group were added together to give a sum of peer marks for the whole group. This was then used to calculate the proportion of peer marks that each student had obtained. The final mark for each student was then calculated as this proportion of the total group marks. Although it is possible to get over 100% with this formula we will cap any one student's mark to this maximum. So far this situation has not arisen.

A major advantage of this scheme is that it takes into account whether the students are harsh or lenient markers.

Obviously the system will not work if students fail to return their forms. Consequently the students were told that they would get no marks for their project if they failed to hand the forms in — there was a very high return rate of forms.

The students were much happier with this scheme. The students appreciated being able to reward hard work and penalise freeloaders. There were favourable reports from both the end of module evaluation questionnaires and the staff-student committee meeting. Some of the students with low grades complained but because the group leaders had been instructed to keep attendance registers it was relatively easy to point out to them that they had contributed very little and they usually agreed without further complaint.

This second scheme solved the problems as far as the students were concerned, but there was still a major administrative problem for us relating to the reading of the forms. Although the ICR system was very efficient it relied on the students using legible script and filling all the boxes in correctly. In particular problems occurred when a student failed to give an absent student 0 rather than leave the form blank. Each time the forms were illegible or filled in wrongly, they had to be checked by the operator. With the large numbers of students involved this became very onerous.

 ## YEAR 3 — MOVE THE ADMIN ONLINE

As a result of the problems we have changed the system again this year. This time the students are required to enter their marks for their colleagues using a web-based form. The web forms have built in validation so that they cannot be submitted with any blank fields. Each student is sent an email giving them a unique URL code which has been generated from their matriculation number and name. This URL gives them access to their own individual website which has a web form with a list of their other group members and spaces to enter their marks.

The system is currently working well. It is important to emphasise that we have only been able to cope with running a successful peer-assessment scheme for such a large class, because we have had the assistance of a dedicated IT specialist and suitable technology. The programming required for generating the web forms and using Excel to calculate the marks is not extremely advanced. It can be done in a number of ways, but does require someone with suitable experience.

 ## FURTHER DEVELOPMENT

One factor that perhaps could be improved is what we tell the students about how their final grade is calculated. In their instructions for the Lifestyle Assignment they are told:

"You will be allocated a mark according to the overall group performance (i.e. a mark for the poster and the debate) *and* to how your own group has assessed your contribution to the group tasks".

This seems to be perfectly adequate but there are always a few students who like to know precisely how their mark is calculated. On reflection following writing up this case study, in future we will use the explanation given here as information on the students' Level 1 Biology website.

5

Peer-assessment of practical write-ups using an explicit marking schedule

IAN HUGHES

 ## BACKGROUND AND RATIONALE

This method of peer-assessment was introduced into a first year pharmacology programme with 50–160 students per year and has also been used with 2nd year medical students (275). Many of the learning objectives were particular to the content of each of the exercises to which peer-assessment was applied but, in addition, some generic problems and learning objectives were addressed by use of this method of peer-assessment:

- *Utilization of feedback.* There was little evidence that students took any notice of (or even read) the material laboriously written on each practical by members of staff. This method provides each student with a full explanation of what should have been done. Every students gets excellent and timely feedback to which, by the nature of the process, they must pay attention.

- *Development of critical evaluation skills.* Students have to make judgements about the quality of their work to achieve the standards to which they aspire and in order to time-manage their activities. This is not something which comes easy to all students and practice with critical evaluation in the early part of a course helps prepare students for what they will need to do later. The ability to be critical of your own work and that of others is a valuable transferable skill. Surveys show graduates in first employment have to assess the work of others surprisingly early in their jobs. Graduates are often not prepared for this.

- *Better understanding of the material.* Students, like everyone else, need a better understanding to assess something than to produce it. This is particularly true if dealing with somebody else's work where the words and their order are not those you yourself would have used.

- *Improved learning.* This method provides a second look at the material covered. Learning is improved and reinforced by the feedback resulting from participation in the assessment process.

- *Motivation.* This method enables students to see the standard others achieve and where their own work may be improved. This is more powerful than seeing a 'perfect answer' written by a member of academic staff ('of course they can produce a good answer or they wouldn't be on the academic staff!'). Seeing your peers are doing a much better job than you are even when subject to the same pressures is a powerful spur for improvement.

- *Developing independence.* Students confront the 'personal relationship' issue and learn to make assessments independent of any personal relationship. This requires a very different attitude to that which many students have on leaving school ("always look after your mates").

- *Significant reduction in marking time.* The time involved in marking practical write-ups each week was becoming unsustainable as student numbers increased. Using peer-assessment 250 or more practical write-ups can be marked in one hour.

 ## 'HOW TO DO IT'

The task for the students was to provide a write-up, following a set of instructions, of a scheduled laboratory practical or computer simulated experiment. This practical schedule usually included some questions to test the students' understanding of the material. Written answers to these questions were required as part of the practical write-up.

The write-ups are handed in by a published deadline and there are penalties for being late. Work presented by the deadline is stamped as being received (this stops students slipping late write-ups into the marking session). Split groups may have different deadlines providing they are not too far apart. Time is set aside in the timetable (1 hour) for a marking session and it is made clear that attendance is compulsory, any student missing (without good reason) the marking session looses half the marks they are assigned. It is important to be firm about this as if 200 students do the work and only 120 turn up to the marking session *you* have to mark the other 80 write-ups! At the marking session, having previously explained the advantages of peer-marking, I distribute the write-ups and a record sheet on which the marker fills in their name, the name of the student being marked, the final mark awarded and signs to accept responsibility. An explicit marking schedule is distributed. I emphasise the need for silence during marking and enforce it. I then go through the marking schedule step by step explaining, with pre-prepared slides or acetates, how things should be done, what graphs should look like etc.

Students annotate the write-up they are marking as appropriate and decide what proportion of the marks allocated for each point should be awarded for the material presented. Students asking if a certain wording is worth x or y marks are told they must make the decision from the information they have. Students total the marks awarded, fill in and sign the record sheet. The write-ups, marking schedule and record sheet are collected so marks can be recorded and then the write-up and marking schedule are made available for collection by the owner. Students are told that a portion of the write-ups will be check marked by staff and that any student who feels they had been marked unfairly could have their write-up re-marked by a member of academic staff (less than 2% do so).

 ADVICE ON USING THIS APPROACH

Generally, for students, the process of self-assessment is easier to perform than peer-assessment. I often make the first exposure one of self-assessment and then progress to peer-assessment. It is easier to find key words and phrases in work you have done yourself since you know where everything is. This makes the assessment process easier. However, there is a tendency to assess what you meant to write rather than what is actually there. In addition there is a greater potential for cheating as it has been known for students to fill in or change material in their own submitted work while assessing it. However, self-marking does provide an easy introduction to peer-marking and this can be useful.

Not all practical work is easily amenable to this method as it really hinges on the task set. Work resulting from following a practical schedule is readily peer-assessed. The same measurements have been made with similar data obtained and processed the same way. The write-up needs to follow a specified format that controls the order in which material is presented and the type of data presentation (e.g. present the data in a table, draw a graph etc.). This enables an explicit marking schedule to be provided with the material broken down into small pieces, each of which is associated with specific criteria or requirements for marks to be awarded. Thus, work in year 1/2 is more likely to fulfil these requirements.

Work resulting from a task like 'Describe an ideal vehicle' is not easily peer-assessed except at the very broadest level, since 'vehicle' may have been taken to mean different things (storage vehicle, transport vehicle, communication vehicle or vehicle in which to dissolve something) and 'ideal' will depend on where the writer is coming from. The marking schedule to meet all possibilities is either so general as to ignore specific content or so extensive that it takes too long to write and is very difficult for students to follow. Final year level work, where several completely different but valid approaches to the task could have been taken, is therefore difficult to peer-assess using the simple methods described here. Likewise, "Is the work well presented?" is not a reasonable question as there are no specific criteria associated with it. Each student may

make a judgement based on different criteria and considerable personal preference may come into the assessment.

The practical work needs to be done by the student body over a short period of time so the assessment session can follow in a timely manner. If six weeks elapse between the first student doing the work and the assessment process the students will have forgotten what it was all about. Work done as part of a 'circussed' set of exercises is therefore not suitable as the first group cannot be assessed as soon as they have completed the task (or they will pass the answers on to others) and it may be several weeks before all students have done all the tasks, without getting any feedback on their performance.

The task set needs to change from year to year. If an identical task is set each year the marking schedules will get passed on and while student performance might improve year on year this is only because they are copying out last year's marking schedule. I currently have a set of three versions of each exercise which I rotate each year and have not yet any evidence that the material gets passed on. I have had instances where students handed in a write-up based on *last* year's exercise data and then complained that I had not warned them that the exercise was different year on year!

 TROUBLESHOOTING

Don't think your students are going to enjoy peer-assessment! Many believe assessment is the job of the teacher ("don't you get paid for this?"), many complain that peer-assessment is hard work ("you have to think and make judgements"), and that it's tiring ("I'm really bushed at the end of a marking session"). Some find it difficult to concentrate for a whole hour. Some believe student markers are unfair or inaccurate. The reasons for introducing peer- or self-marking need to be explained to students if it is to be introduced without resentment. See Figure 1 for documentation that has been used effectively in preparing students.

Silence in class during the marking process is imperative. Otherwise students will miss your explanations, ask for repetitions or misunderstand what was required and the marking session will take forever. In an ideal world, it might be possible to allow or encourage students to discuss and compare what is written in the material they are marking; but when I have tried this, the time taken was greatly prolonged and while some students were bored, others demanded more time. Not a good idea in practice; unless there is only a small amount of material to mark and no absolute deadline to complete the process by.

Figure 1. Part of a document used in preparing students for peer-marking, explaining the benefits to them

Student Guide to Peer-Assessment of Practicals

Why are we doing this?

You should get several things out of this method of assessment which may be new to you:

1. It is an open marking system; therefore you can see what was required and how to improve your work.

2. You see mistakes others make and therefore can avoid them; you also see the standard achieved by others and can set your own work in the spectrum of marks.

3. You get a full explanation of the practical and how you should have processed the data and done the discussion. Therefore your information and understanding is improved.

4. You get practise in assessing others and their work. You will need this skill quite early in a career and you will need to come to terms with the problem of bias; someone who is a good friend may have done poor work; it can be disturbing to have to give them a poor mark.

5. In assessing others you should acquire the ability to stand back from your own work and assess that as well. This is an essential ability in a scientist; an unbiased and objective assessment of the standards you have achieved in your own work. Once you are away from the teacher/pupil relationship (i.e. leave university) you will be the person who decides if a piece of work is good enough to be considered as finished and passed to your boss.

The method of marking adopted in this module is designed with the above factors in mind.

 DOES IT WORK?

The published evidence (Hughes, 1995 and 2001) indicates the students on average produced better write-ups when using peer-assessment than they did when staff marking was used. The data demonstrate that this is not due to students being easier markers.

Peer-assessment saves an enormous amount of staff time, provides excellent feedback and achieves many of the points bulleted above. Marking accuracy is often queried but students can always check their mark against their copy of the marking schedule and appeal to the tutor if they are dissatisfied. To test reproducibility of marking three copies of the same practical were peer-marked independently by students as part of the normal marking session. The marks awarded differed by only 3% demonstrating the consistency of the marking process. In addition, I have, using the same marking schedule, personally marked several samples of peer-marked work. In every case the discrepancy was less than 5%. Confidence can be placed in peer-generated marks which can therefore be used as part of the marks which contribute to final module grades. External examiners have not objected to the use of peer-assessed marks in this way.

Several colleagues have started to utilize this method and no new problems or difficulties have been encountered.

 ACCOMPANYING MATERIAL

The accompanying website to this guide (http://www.heabioscience.academy.ac.uk/TeachingGuides/) contains an extended version of this case study and the following additional material:

- an explicit peer-marking schedule;

- peer-assessment of oral presentations.

6

Writing and reviewing an article for a scientific magazine — a peer/ self-assessment exercise

ROB REED

 BACKGROUND AND RATIONALE

This exercise forms part of a second year module in research methods and scientific communication, taught to classes of 60–90 bioscience students. Students can find such topics rather dry and, as a result, the taught sessions rely heavily on workbooks and worksheets to cover the syllabus, which includes: locating and evaluating sources; primary and secondary literature; style and layout; the peer review system and its role in scientific publication; citation and referencing. The assignment requires students to apply the knowledge they have gained in the taught sessions to a short exercise, to satisfy the following learning outcomes:

- Use relevant methods to locate and interpret research information in the primary scientific literature.

- Use appropriate forms of scientific communication, in this module and in other modules within the programme.

 'HOW TO DO IT'

The following steps describe the principal stages:

1. Having come to appreciate the difference between a primary and secondary source in the workshop sessions, students are instructed to select an interesting, recent paper from the primary scientific literature (published within the last few months, to avoid any possibility of plagiarism from previous years). Each student selects a different article (a sign-up sheet on the notice board enables students to check which papers have been selected and rewards those students who get off to a quick start!).

2. Students make a photocopy or printout of the paper: this is needed by their peer reviewer and must also be handed in along with their assignment.

3. Each student then prepares a brief article (400–500 words) about their chosen paper in the style of the 'This Week' section of *New Scientist* magazine. Students are told that their article should conform in general style and approach to the examples found in any copy of *New Scientist* (examples are also available from the website: http://www.newscientist.com) and they are given other guidance on layout (e.g. typed double-spaced, 12 point font, to include a word count, a full citation of the primary source is required, etc.).

4. Pairs of students then exchange articles and review each other's work, using an evaluation sheet very similar in overall style to that used by scientific journals. The reviewer must assess the article and (i) decide whether the article is acceptable without change or whether minor/major revision is required (ii) provide specific feedback on any points raised, e.g. by writing comments on the article, or as a numbered sequence, cross-referenced against the article. The reviewer is also given a copy of the original article, so he/she can see whether there are any omissions, etc.

5. Student reviewers then return the article and evaluation sheet to the original author, who has then to consider their response to the review, using a response form. Students must decide whether to (i) modify their article, where they feel that the reviewer's comments are appropriate and (ii) prepare a written response to each of the points raised by the reviewer. In this way, they are given a hands-on introduction to a process similar to that used for peer review of a primary scientific article. Students are also encouraged to reflect on their own work (self-evaluation), especially if they feel that their reviewer has been "lightweight" in providing feedback.

6. Students must then hand in for final assessment (i) the photocopy/printout of the original paper (ii) a copy of their original (unreviewed) article (iii) a copy of their reviewed article along with the reviewer's comments and

evaluation sheet (iv) their response to the review/evaluation and (v) a copy of the final version of their article.

7. The exercise is then marked on the following basis.

- The quality of the original (unreviewed) version of the article, as an exercise in presenting key information from the original paper in an appropriate and accessible style, with due regard for the target audience (general readership of *New Scientist* magazine) — 30% of the overall mark.

- The student's response to peer review (and/or self-evaluation), as evidenced by (i) the changes made to the original version in producing the final version and (ii) the response sheet, dealing with reviewer's comments — 30% of the overall mark.

- The student's effectiveness as a peer reviewer, based on (i) written comments on their partner's article and (ii) the evaluation sheet of their partner's article — 40% of the overall mark.

 ## ADVICE ON USING THIS APPROACH

It is essential that students are given clear instructions in writing at the outset of the exercise, to support the oral explanation given during the class. I have found it necessary to provide quite detailed guidance (for example, many students didn't understand the concept of double-spacing, thinking that this meant having two spaces between each word!). The guidelines now explain that a space equivalent to two lines is needed in the printed version to give sufficient room for the reviewer to provide handwritten comments, along with step-wise instructions on how to set up MS Word to provide double-spaced text). I have also found it useful to provide the students with a detailed checklist of all of the items required for submission, since it can be a little confusing (they have to realise, for example, that their work as a reviewer will be handed in by their partner, and that I will separately assess this aspect of their work, and then collate the marks).

It can sometimes be a little difficult keeping track of which students are working together — I ask them to sign up in pairs at the outset, and not to switch partners without informing me. I allow them to select their own partners, and I tell them that they should not regard this in any way as a "soft option", since I will have oversight of the whole process, and

that students who simply give their partner an undeservedly positive review will score poorly in that aspect of the exercise!

 ## TROUBLESHOOTING

Sometimes students will work in threes, rather than pairs — in such instances, each person reviews the work of a different person to their own reviewer. It works just as well this way, and is an alternative approach, avoiding reciprocal peer-assessment.

In occasional instances, there is a problem with one of the team members (e.g. where a student does not return the reviewed article by the specified date, or where someone is ill during the programme) — such cases have been dealt with on an individual basis by either (ii) reassigning group members or (ii) asking one student to perform a second (unassessed) review, so that all elements of the process are covered.

It can be a little tricky marking the various aspects of different people's work at different times — my approach has been to mark the review (second person's mark) at the same time as the original and final versions of the article (first person's mark) to ensure continuity in reading the article, and to use a pre-printed feedback sheet with a number of general comments to provide overall feedback, as well as a mark for each component. This structured approach works well with a large group of students.

 ## DOES IT WORK?

Student feedback is usually positive for this aspect of the programme — students generally regard it as an interesting exercise, and a welcome change from more traditional essays and similar written assignments.

FURTHER DEVELOPMENTS

It has run successfully in its present form for the past five years. To date, the peer/self-assessment component has been restricted to a broad overall evaluation, based on written feedback, rather than a quantitative numerical mark/grade. One aspect that could be introduced relatively easily would be to ask students to provide a numerical mark for each of the aspects of the process (e.g. self-assessment of (i) the original article and (ii) the final article, and (iii) peer-assessment of their partner's article. Students would then be able to compare their own assessment marks with those of the lecturer, to see how effectively they can assess their own work and that of others, using the same criteria as those of the teaching staff.

ACCOMPANYING MATERIAL

The accompanying website to this guide (http://www.heabioscience.academy.ac.uk/TeachingGuides/) contains an extended version of this case study and the following additional material:

- student assignment;

- assignment front sheet;

- peer reviewer's evaluation sheet; and

- author's response to peer reviewer's comment.

7

Peer-assessed problem-based case studies

CHARLES BRENNAN, ELIZABETH FOLLAND, RICK PRESTON & NICOLA BLATCHFORD

 BACKGROUND AND RATIONALE

Final Year Food Technology students participate in a real-life problem-based case study. Each case study focuses on a small problem within a larger graduate research project being undertaken by the university with an industrial partner. As such, the project tends to be a blend of the practical use of food technology pilot plant equipment and background theoretical research. Students are allowed to organise their work pattern in order to meet the objectives of the particular project.

The final assessment of the case study is as a group, conference-style, oral presentation. These presentations are exclusively peer-assessed. Time is taken within the module to discuss and devise appropriate marking strategies and descriptors. Thus the students take ownership not only over their working time but also in the style of assessment strategy, giving them greater understanding of learning patterns.

 'HOW TO DO IT'

During the final week of research activity, students are reminded about the mini-conference presentations which are required as their assessment of the case study. Guidance is given on presentation techniques and the use of graphics and IT in presenting information using MS PowerPoint. Examples of previous conference presentations are provided as a benchmark. At the same time, the marking strategy is discussed and the elements of presentation to be assessed, together with the balance of marks associated with each element, are agreed within the group. This process is mediated by the academic; however the students lead the discussion and formulate the marking criteria.

On the day of the student presentations, evaluation sheets are distributed amongst the group and the process of peer-assessment is reinforced. The presentation evaluation sheets are graded on a scale 1–9 using the criteria already agreed on. A total of 10 criteria relating to both product and process are used, such as relevance of information supplied, evidence of sound laboratory practice, evidence of teamwork, timekeeping, readability of slides and amount of information supplied.

Students are then expected to evaluate each groups' performance (according to the criteria already laid down), and any additional information about a groups' performance is noted on the evaluation form. At the end of the series of presentations, all evaluation sheets are collected in by the academic. Evaluation sheets obtained in this exercise are then scrutinised by the academic and the marks allocated to each group (for every element of the assessment) are fed into a database. The final mark for each specific element of the exercise is given as the mean awarded to the group by their peers, and the overall mark is derived according to the marking criteria as agreed by the students.

Follow-up workshops are used to disseminate good practice to students and to evaluate student perception of the process.

 TIPS/THINGS TO LOOK OUT FOR

Staff need to be willing to explain (openly) how and why student assessment criteria are set. This facilitates the students' understanding of developing their own marking criteria and leads into the idea of peer-assessment. Sometimes the actual idea of peer-assessment is so strange to the students that additional time needs to be spent in reassuring them of the fairness of such schemes, and the importance of treating the process professionally.

? DOES IT WORK?

The use of peer-assessment in this case study benefits the students. Although there may be a slight reluctance to use peer-assessment for the assignment initially (sometimes students express a wish that the assignment is evaluated by academics, following usual guidelines). However, the students do accept their roles in the assessment procedure and act responsibly. Through completing the assessment they do learn how to reflect on the work of their peers, how to assess and evaluate work separate from personal friendships, and how to accept positive criticisms regarding the quality of their own work. Indeed, it is interesting that the process also allows the students to reflect on their own learning styles and choices of appropriate communication tools.

As such the case study is extremely useful in developing critical evaluation of their own compositions, and a greater autonomy over their working practices. This development of self-evaluation, and self-worth, is noteworthy when you also take into account the students' greater awareness of the use of their skills and knowledge acquired so far, in problem-solving real-life situations.

FURTHER DEVELOPMENTS

Further developments may be to devise workshops specifically aimed at introducing the principles and aims of peer-assessment. This would have the advantage of reducing student reluctance to participate in such exercises, and also help with their understanding of assessment marking strategies. A result of such could be their ability to better manage their own assessment achievements in modules.

REFERENCES

Adams, C. and King, K. (1995) Towards a framework for self-assessment. *Innovations in Education and Training International*, 32(4), 336–343.

Barnett, R. (2000) Supercomplexity and the Curriculum. *Studies in Higher Education*, 25(3), 255–265.

Biggs, J. (1996) Assessing learning quality: reconciling institutional, staff and educational demands. *Assessment and Evaluation in Higher Education*, 21(1), 5–15.

Biggs, J. (1999) *Teaching for quality learning at university*. Buckingham, UK: Society for Research into Higher Education and the Open University.

Boud, D. (1986) *Implementing student self-assessment*. Sydney, Australia: Higher Education Research and Development Society of Australia.

Boud, D. (1988) Moving towards autonomy. In *Developing Student Autonomy in Learning*, (ed) Boud, D., pp 17–39. London, UK: Kogan Page.

Boud, D. (1989) The role of self-assessment in student grading. *Assessment & Evaluation in Higher Education*, 14(1), 20–30.

Boud, D. (1995) Assessment and learning: contradictory or complementary. In *Assessment for Learning in Higher Education*, (ed) Knight, P., pp 35–48. London, UK: Kogan Page.

Boud, D. (2000) Sustainable assessment: rethinking assessment for the learning society. *Studies in Continuing Education*, 22(2), 151–167.

Boud, D. and Falchikov, N. (1989) Quantitative studies of student self-assessment in higher education; a critical analysis of findings. *Higher Education*, 18, 529–549.

Boud, D. and Falchikov, N. (2004) Beyond formative and summative assessment: developing a new agenda for assessment for lifelong learning. Paper presented at *Assessment 2004 Beyond Intuition, the Second Biannual Joint Northumbria/EARLI SIG Assessment Conference*, University of Bergen, Norway, June 23–25 2004.

Brew, A. (1995) How does self-assessment relate to ideas about learning? In *Enhancing Learning through Self Assessment*, (ed) Boud, D., pp 24–35. London, UK and Philadelphia: Kogan Page.

Brown, S. and Glasner, A. (2003) *Assessment Matters in Higher Education: Choosing and Using Diverse Approaches*, 3rd edition. Buckingham, UK: The Society for Research into Higher Education and Open University Press.

Brown, G., Bull, J. and Pendlebury, M. (1997) *Assessing Student Learning in Higher Education*. London, UK: Routledge.

Brown, S., Sambell, K. and McDowell, L. (1998) What do students think about peer assessment? In *Peer Assessment in Practice*, (ed) Brown, S., 107–112. Birmingham, UK: Staff and Educational Development Association (SEDA).

Butcher, A. C., Stefani, L. A. J. and Tariq, V. N. (1995) Analysis of peer-, self- and staff-assessment in group work. *Assessment in Education*, 2(2), 165–185.

Candy, P., Harri-Augstein, S. and Thomas, L. (1985) Debriefing in experience-based learning. In *Reflection: Turning Experience into Learning*, (eds) Boud, D., Keogh, R. and Walker, D., 100–116. London, UK: Kogan Page.

Chanock, K. (2000) Comments on essays: do students understand what tutors write? *Teaching in Higher Education*, 5(1) 95–105.

Cheng, W. and Warren, M. (1997) Having second thoughts: students perceptions before and after a peer assessment exercise. *Studies in Higher Education*, 22(2), 233–239.

Cheng, W. and Warren, M. (1999) Peer and teacher assessment of the oral and written tasks of a group project. *Assessment & Evaluation in Higher Education*, 24(3), 301–314.

Claxton, G. (1995) What kind of learning does self-assessment drive? Developing a 'nose' for quality: comments on Klenowski. *Assessment in Education*, 2(2), 339–343.

Cook, A. and Rushton, B.S. (1995) An information technology course for biological science students taught through peer tutoring. In *Enhancing student learning through peer tutoring in higher education. Section three: Implementing*, (eds) Griffiths, S., Houston, K. and Lazenbatt, A. pp. 15–21 Coleraine, UK: University of Ulster.

Cowan, J. (2002) *On Becoming an Innovative University Teacher Reflection in Action* 4th Edition. Buckingham, UK: The Society for Research into Higher Education and Open University Press.

Cowan, J., Joyce, J., McPherson, D and Weedon, E. (1999) Self -
assessment of reflective journaling — and its effect on learning outcomes. *4th Northumbria Assessment Conference*, 1–3 September 1999, University of Northumbria, UK.

Dearing, R. (1997). *Higher Education in the Learning Society*. Norwich, UK: HMSO.

Dochy, F., Segers, M. and Sluijsman. D. (1999) The use of self-peer and co-assessment in higher education: a review. *Studies in Higher Education*, 24(3), 331–350.

Drew, S. (2001) Students perceptions of what helps them learn and develop in higher education. *Teaching in Higher Education*, 6(3), 309–331.

Edwards, A. Knight, P. T. (1995) *Assessing Competence in Higher Education*. London, UK: Kogan Page.

Ecclestone, K. (2001) 'I know a 2:1 when I see it': understanding criteria for degree classification in franchised university programmes. *Journal of Further and Higher Education*, 25(3), 301–313.

Elwood, J. and Klenowski, V. (2002) Creating communities of shared practice: the challenges of assessment use in learning and teaching. *Assessment and Evaluation in Higher Education*, 27(3), 243–256.

Falchikov, N. (1995) Peer feedback marking: developing peer assessment. *Innovations in Education and Training International*, 32(2), 175–187.

Falchikov, N. (2001) *Learning Together. Peer Tutoring in Higher Education*. London, UK: Routledge.

Falchikov, N. (2003) Involving students in assessment. *Psychology Learning and Teaching*, 3(2), 102–108.

Falchikov, N. and Boud, D. (1989) Student self-assessment in higher education: a meta-analysis. *Review of Educational Research*, 59(4), 431–470.

Falchikov, N. and Magin, D. (1997) Detecting gender bias in peer marking of students' group process work. *Assessment and Evaluation in Higher Education*, 22(4), 385–396.

Falchikov, N. and Goldfinch, J. (2000) Student peer assessment in higher education: a meta-analysis comparing peer and teacher marks. *Review of Educational Research*, 70(3), 287–322.

Freeman, M. (1995) Peer assessment by groups of group work. *Assessment and Evaluation in Higher Education*, 20(3), 289–299.

Freeman, R. and Lewis, R. (1998) *Planning and Implementing Assessment*. London, UK: Kogan Page.

Fry, H., Ketteridge, S and Marshall, S (1999) *A Handbook for Teaching and Learning in Higher Education*. London, UK: Kogan Page.

Gabb, R. (1981) Playing the project game. *Assessment and Evaluation in Higher Education*, 6(1), 26–48.

Gielen, S., Dochy, F. and Dierick, S. (2003) New insights into learning and teaching and their implication for assessment. In *Optimising New Modes of Assessment: in Search of Qualities and Standards* (eds) Segers, M., Dochy, F. and Cascallar, E., pp. 37–54. London, UK: Kluwer Academic Publishers.

Goldfinch, J. (1994) Further developments in peer assessment of group projects. *Assessment and Evaluation in Higher Education*, 19(1), 29–34.

Griffiths, S., Houston, K. and Lazenbatt, A. (1995) *Enhancing student learning through peer tutoring in higher education. Section three: Implementing*. Coleraine, UK: University of Ulster.

Heron, J. (1988) Assessment revisited. In *Developing Student Autonomy in Learning* (ed) Boud, D., pp. 77–90. London, UK: Kogan Page.

Heron, J. (1992) The politics of facilitation: balancing facilitator authority and learning autonomy. In *Empowerment through Experiential Learning: Exploration of Good Practice* (eds) Mulligan, J. and Griffin, C., pp. 66–75. London, UK: Kogan Page.

Higgs, J. (1988) Planning learning experiences to promote autonomous learning. In *Developing Student Autonomy in Learning* (ed) Boud, D., pp 40–58. London, UK: Kogan Page.

Hinett, K. (1995) Fighting the assessment war: the idea of assessment-in-learning. *Quality in Higher Education*, 1(3), 211–222.

Hughes, I. E. (1995) Peer assessment of student practical reports and its influence on learning and skill acquisition. *Capability*, 1, 39–43.

Hughes, I. E. (2001) But isn't this what you're paid for? The pros and cons of self- and peer-assessment. *Planet*, 2: 20–23.

Hughes, I. E. and Large, B. J. (1993) Staff and peer-group assessment of oral communication skills. *Studies in Higher Education*, 18(3), 379–385.

Jackson, N. and Ward, R. (2004) A fresh perspective on progress files — a way of representing complex learning and achievement in higher education. *Assessment and Evaluation in Higher Education*, 29(4) 423–449.

Klenowski, V. (1995) Student self-evaluation process in student-centred teaching and learning contexts of Australia and England. *Assessment in Education*, 2(2), 145–163.

Knight, P. (2001) A Briefing on Key Concepts: Formative and Summative, Criterion and Norm-referenced Assessment. *LTSN Generic Centre Assessment Series No. 7*. York, UK: Learning and Teaching Support Network.

Knight, P. (2002) Summative assessment in higher education: practices in disarray. *Studies in Higher Education*, 27(3), 275–286.

Knight, P. and Yorke, M. (2003) *Assessment, Learning and Employability*. Berkshire, UK: Open University Press.

Kolb, D. A. (1984) *Experiential Learning. Experience as the Source of Learning and Development*. New Jersey, USA: Prentice Hall.

Kuit, J. A., Reay, G. and Freeman, R. (2001) Experiences of reflective teaching. *Active Learning in Higher Education*, 2(2), 128–142.

Lejk, M. and Wyvill, M. (2002) Peer assessment of contributions to a group project: student attitudes to holistic and category-based approaches. *Assessment and Evaluation in Higher Education*, 27(6), 569–577.

Li, L. K. Y. (2001) Some refinements on peer assessment of group projects. *Assessment and Evaluation in Higher Education*, 26(1), 5–18.

MacDonald, J. (2004) Developing competent e-learners: the role of assessment. *Assessment and Evaluation in Higher Education*, 29(2), 215–226.

Maclellan, E. (2001) Assessment for learning; the differing perceptions of tutors and students. *Assessment and Evaluation in Higher Education*, 26(4), 307–318.

Magin, D. (1993) Should student peer ratings be used as part of summative assessment? *Higher Educational Research and Development*, 16, 537–542.

Magin, D. (2001) Reciprocity as a source of bias in multiple peer assessment of group work. *Studies in Higher Education*, 26(1), 53–63.

Marton, F. and Saljo, R. (1976) On qualitative differences in learning: I — outcome and process. *British Journal of Educational Psychology*, 46, 4–11.

Miller, J. P (2003) The effect of scoring criteria specificity on self- and peer-assessment . *Assessment and Evaluation in Higher Education*, 28(4), 383–394.

Moon, J. (2001) Reflection in Higher Education Learning. PDP Working Paper 4. York, UK: LTSN Generic Centre, http://www.ltsn.ac.uk/embedded_object.asp?id=17305&prompt=yes&filename=PDP012 (accessed 5th August, 2004).

Nieweg, N. (2004) Case study: innovative assessment and curriculum design. *Assessment and Evaluation in Higher Education*, 29(2), 203–214.

Ngu, A. H. H., Shepherd, J. and Magin, D. (1995) Engineering the 'Peers' system: the development of a computer-assisted approach to peer assessment. *Research and Development in Higher Education*, 18, 582–587.

Orsmond, P., Merry, S. and Reiling, K. (1996). The Importance of Marking Criteria in the Use of Peer Assessment. *Assessment and Evaluation in Higher Education*, 21(3), pp 239–250.

Orsmond, P., Merry, S. and Reiling, K. (1997). A study in self-assessment: tutor and students' perceptions of performance criteria. *Assessment and Evaluation in Higher Education*, 22(4), 357–369.

Orsmond, P., Merry, S. and Reiling, K. (2000). The use of student-derived marking criteria in peer- and self-assessment. *Assessment and Evaluation in Higher Education*, 25(1) pp. 23–39.

Orsmond, P., Merry, S. and Reiling, K. (2002) The use of exemplars and formative feedback when using student derived marking criteria in peer- and self-assessment. *Assessment and Evaluation in Higher Education*, 27 (4) 309–323.

Orsmond, P., Merry, S., and Callaghan, A. C. (2004) Implementation of a formative assessment model incorporating peer- and self-assessment. *Innovations in Education and Training International* (in press).

Pereira, M. (1999) My reflective practice as research. *Teaching in Higher Education*, 4(3) 339–354.

Pond, K., Ul-haq, R. and Wade, W. (1995) Peer review: a precursor to peer-assessment. *Innovations in Education and Training International*, 32(4), 314–323.

Race, P. (1998) Practical pointers on peer assessment. In *Peer Assessment in Practice*, (ed) Brown, S., pp. 113–122. Birmingham, UK: Staff and Educational Development Association (SEDA).

Ramaprasad, A. (1983) On the definition of feedback. *Behavioural Sciences*, 28, pp. 4–13.

Rogers, C. R. (2003) *Client-Centered Therapy*. London, UK: Constable and Robinson.

Rushton, C., Ramsey, P. and Rada, R. (1993) Peer assessment in a collaborative hypermedia environment: A case study. *Journal of Computer-Based Instruction*, 20(3), 75–80.

Rust, C., Price, M. and O'Donovan, B. (2003) Improving students' learning by developing their understanding of assessment criteria and processes. *Assessment and Evaluation in Higher Education* 28(2), 147–164.

Sadler, D. R. (1989) Specifying and promulgating achievement standards. *Oxford Review of Education*, 13, 191–209.

Sambell, K. and McDowell, L. (1998). The construction of the hidden curriculum: messages and meanings in the assessment of student learning. *Assessment and Evaluation in Higher Education*, 23(4), 391–402.

Sambell, K., McDowell, L. and Brown, S. (1997) "But is it fair?": an exploratory study of student perceptions of the consequential validity of assessment. *Studies in Educational Evaluation*, 23(4), 349–371.

Schelfhout, W., Dochy, F. and Janssens, S. (2004) The use of self, peer and teacher assessment as a feedback system in a learning environment aimed at fostering skills of cooperation in an entrepreneurial context. *Assessment and Evaluation in Higher Education*, 29(2), 177–201.

Schön, D. (1983) *The Reflective Practitioner: how professionals think in action*. New York, USA: Basic Books Inc.

Segers, M. and Dochy, F. (2001) New assessment forms in problem-based learning: the value-added of the students' perspective. *Studies in Higher Education*, 26(3), 327–343.

Sivan, A (2000) The implementation of peer assessment: an action research approach. *Assessment in Education*, 7(2), 193–212.

Sluijsmans, D. (2002) Establishing learning effects with integrated peer assessment tasks, http://www.ilt.ac.uk/1204.asp (restricted access).

Stefani, L. A. J. (1992) Comparison of collaborative self, peer and tutor assessment in a biochemistry practical. *Biochemical Education*, 20(3), 148–151.

Stefani, L. A. J. (1994) Peer, self and tutor assessment: relative reliabilities. *Studies in Higher Education*, 19(1), 69–75.

Sullivan, K. and Hall, C. (1997) Introducing students to self-assessment. *Assessment and Evaluation in Higher Education*, 22(3), 289–305.

Sutherland, P. (1992) *Cognitive Development Today: Piaget and his Critics*. London, UK: Paul Chapman.

Tan, K. H. K. (2004) Does student self-assessment empower or discipline students? *Assessment and Evaluation in Higher Education*, 29(6), 651–662.

Taras, M. (2001) The use of tutor feedback and student self-assessment in summative assessment tasks: towards transparency for students and for tutors. *Assessment and Evaluation in Higher Education*, 26(6), 605–614.

Taras, M. (2003) To feedback or not to feedback in student self-assessment. *Assessment and Evaluation in Higher Education*, 28(5), 549–565.

Topping, K. J. (2003) Self- and peer-assessment in school and university: reliability, validity and utility. In *Optimising New modes of Assessment in Search of Qualities and Standards*, (eds) Segers, M., Dochy, F. and Cascallar, E., pp. 55–87. London, UK: Kluwer Academic Publishers.

Topping, K. J., Smith, E. F., Swanson, I. and Elliot, A. (2000) Formative peer assessment of academic writing between postgraduate students. *Assessment and Evaluation in Higher Education*, 25(2) 150–169.

Vygotsky, L. S. (1978) *Mind in Society*. Cambridge, USA: Harvard University Press.

Wood, D. (1988) *How Children Think and Learn*, 2nd edition. Oxford, UK: Basil Blackwell Ltd.

Wood, D., Bruner, J. and Ross, G. (1976) The role of tutoring in problem solving. *Journal of Child Psychology and Psychiatry*, 17, 89–100.